THE RAINDROP'S GOSPEL

THE RAINDROP'S GOSPEL:

THE TRIALS OF ST. JEROME AND ST. PAULA

A Novel in Verse

MAURYA SIMON

Cover art: "Saint Jerome" by Caravaggio. Galleria Borghese, Rome

Page 9: "St. Jerome in his Study" by Albrecht Dürer. British Museum, London

Page 41: "The Departure of Saint Paula and Saint Eustochium
for the Holy Land" by Giuseppe Bottani.
The Metropolitan Museum of Art, New York, New York

Front cover photo by freeparking via flickr

Author photo by Robert Falk

Book design by Joel A. Bass

ISBN: 978-1-932-41834-7 (paper)
ISBN: 978-1-932-41837-8 (cloth)

Elixir Press
PO Box 27029
Denver, Colorado 80227

www.ElixirPress.com

Elixir Press is a nonprofit literary organization.

Library of Congress Cataloging-in-Publication Data

Simon, Maurya, 1950-
The raindrop's gospel : the trials of St. Jerome And St. Paula :
a novel in verse / by Maurya Simon.
p. cm.
Includes bibliographical references.
ISBN 978-1-932418-34-7
1. Jerome, Saint, d. 419 or 20--Poetry. 2. Paula, Saint, 347-404--Poetry.
I. Title.
PS3569.I4827F35 2009
811'.54--dc22
2009026582

Also by Maurya Simon:

The Enchanted Room

Days of Awe

Speaking in Tongues

The Golden Labyrinth

A Brief History of Punctuation

Ghost Orchid

WEAVERS

Cartographies

Table of Contents

For Robert, my perpetual conspirator

And for my own St. Paula and Dan Van Clapp, Master of Whirligigs

Genealogies

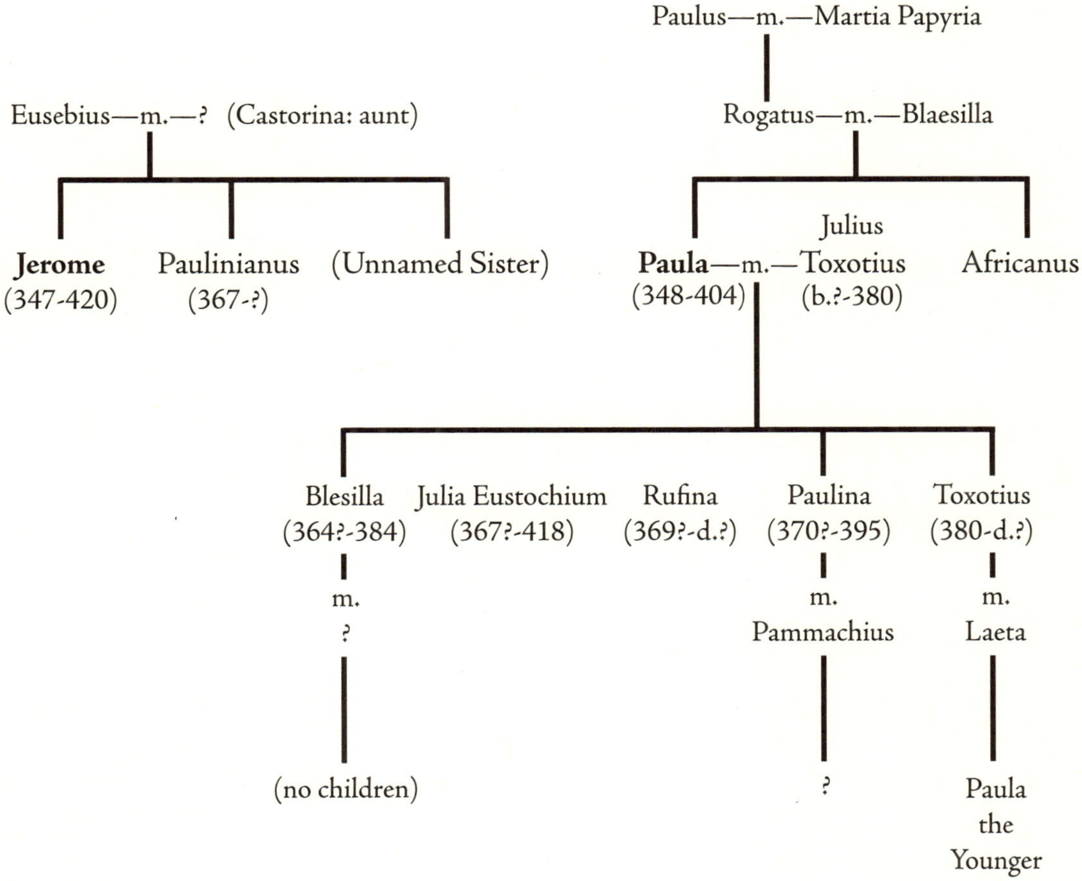

Chronologies of the Lives of St. Jerome and St. Paula

347 C.E. – Eusebius Hieronymus (a.k.a. Sophronius, later St. Jerome) was born in Stridon, Dalmatia (probably near modern Ljubljana, Slovenia) of affluent Christian parents. His father is also called Eusebius (Greek: "piety"). Jerome never refers to his mother by name in his *Letters*, but he refers to his brother, Paulianus (Paulinian), to an unnamed sister, to his foster brother, Bonosus, and to his maternal aunt, Castorina.

359 – Hieronymus is sent to Rome at the age of twelve to study Latin grammar (with Aelius Donatus), rhetoric (with Victorinus), and philosophy. There, during his adolescence, he becomes enamored of Latin literature, lives a hedonistic life, developing tastes for women and fine food, and often frequents the catacombs with his friend, Rufinus, who becomes his theological foe in later years.

360-372 –In 360, Hieronymus is baptized and given the biblical name, "Jerome," probably by Pope Liberius. He spends many years traveling widely in Gaul, Dalmatia, and Italy, and staying in a variety of impermanent residences, while his attraction to monasticism grows, as does his desire to lead an ascetic life.

373 – Jerome begins a trip throughout the East but, due to fatigue and inner turmoil, he stops when he reaches Antioch in 374, where he is the guest of the priest Evagrius. Here Jerome composes his earliest known work, "De septies percussa" ("Concerning Seven Beatings") and, in 375, he suffers his famous dream in which he's dragged before God's tribunal and is accused of being a Ciceronian (a follower of the first century C.E. Roman philosopher), rather than a Christian. He is brutally lashed in the dream, and he vows never again to own or read "pagan" (classical) literature.

374-377 – Jerome spends approximately three years as a hermit in the Syrian desert at Chalcis, searching devoutly for a confirmation of his faith and for inner peace. Here, as a novice ascetic, he suffers from loneliness, from a weak stomach tested by the paltry desert fare, and from the temptations and passions of the flesh. He responds to these trials and torments by praying and fasting incessantly, by studying Syriac, Greek, and Hebrew (this latter language taught to him by various figures, including Baraninas, a Christian convert from Judaism), and by pursuing a wide-ranging correspondence.

378 – Jerome returns to Antioch, where he is known as a significant scholar and monastic figure. Bishop Paulinus ordains him, accepting Jerome's condition that he not be forced to conduct any priestly duties, so he may return to his scholarly pursuits. During this time, he visits the Nazarenes (Jewish Christians) of Beroea to examine their copy of a Hebrew gospel (the Gospel of Matthew).

379-382 – Jerome is ordained a presbyter in Antioch, and he continues his scriptural studies, improves his knowledge of Greek, and translates into Latin fourteen sermons on Old Testament books.

382-384 – Jerome returns to Rome as the secretary to Pope Damasus; he translates some exegetical tracts and translates two sermons from the Song of Solomon. He also revises the Old Latin version of the Gospels, and holds classes for a group of noble Roman widows and virgins, including: Paula and her daughters Julia Eustochium and Blesilla, Blesilla's sister-in-law Furia, Marcella, Marcella's sister Albina and her niece Asella, Felicitas, and Marcellina. He teaches the group the Hebrew text of the Psalms, and serves as their spiritual guide and master. He eventually earns severe criticism from the Church for his questionable relationship with his female coterie, for his castigation of the Roman clergy and its lax monks, and for his corrections to gospel texts. In 385, after Damasus's death, Jerome leaves "Babylon" (Rome) for the Holy Land.

385-389 – Jerome leads Paula, her daughter Eustochium, and several other virgins and widows in a religious and archaeological pilgrimage through Palestine and Egypt. In 386 he settles in Bethlehem (with Paula and Eustochium) where, by 389, he has used Paula's fortune to subsidize the establishment of a monastery for monks, a separate convent for nuns, and a library, built under Jerome's direction. Here he and Paula live, except for brief journeys, for the rest of their lives. His commentary on Ecclesiastes (circa 387) is the first original Latin commentary that relies fully on the Hebrew text.

392-393 – Jerome works on and completes "De viris illustribus ("Concerning Illustrious Men"), in opposition to pagan pride in pagan culture, as well as writing a brilliant but sometimes vulgar diatribe against the claim of equality between virginity and marriage. (Throughout his monastic life, Jerome purportedly suffers from lewd and lustful dreams.) He amasses a considerable library of important biblical texts and commentaries in several languages. Between 391-406, he produces a Latin translation of the Old Testament (the Vulgate edition) based on the original text, a remarkable task. For his Vulgate translations, Jerome utilizes punctuation as a rhetorical system—*per cola et commata* ("by phrases")—relying on earlier texts by Cicero and Demosthenes. Thus, he's a pivotal figure in the development of punctuation.

420 – Jerome dies on September 30th in Bethlehem and is buried beneath the Church of the Nativity, next to Paula's and near Eustochium's graves.

Notes

Medieval and Renaissance portraits of Jerome sometimes (anachronistically) represent him as a cardinal, and they often place him either in a monastic cave or in his monastery library, a lion lying at his feet, and several or all of the following items nearby: a skull, inkwell, and hourglass. When he's not being portrayed as a scholar and theologian, Jerome is often placed in a wilderness landscape and depicted holding a stone, a symbol of his voluntary asceticism and life of harsh penance. As St. Jerome, he serves as the patron saint of librarians and students.

Paula was born circa 348 and died at the age of fifty-six on January 26, 404. Most of what is known about the details of her life is provided by Jerome's *Letters*, in which she figures prominently; however, her side of their correspondence has been lost. She was descended from two of the noblest Roman families of the era, the Scipios and the Gracchi. Paula was married to Toxotious and bore five children (four daughters and one son): Eustochium, Blesilla, Rufina, Paulina, and Toxotious. When she was thirty-two, her husband died, followed shortly by the death of her daughter, Blesilla. This period of extreme sorrow eventually led to her conversion to Christianity and to her lifelong association with Jerome. (The sudden death of Blesilla's husband led Blesilla to convert to Christianity and to a brief period of intensive Hebrew study and of fanatical fasting, the latter practice possibly prompting her own death four months later from a fever.) Rufina and Paulina were teenagers, and Toxotius only a few years old, when their mother, Paula, permanently left Rome for Bethlehem. After Paula's death, her daughter Eustochium assumed leadership of the convent founded by Paula and Jerome in Bethlehem; Eustochium's niece, Paula (the junior Toxotious' daughter and Paula's granddaughter) succeeded Eustochium as the head of this nunnery. Paula (the Elder) is considered the patron saint of widows.

*

Although I use historical facts detailed in various documents pertaining to their actual lives, I focus in this book primarily upon the relationship between Jerome and Paula, as I imagine it, rather than upon the former's religious commentary and treatises.

Though Jerome is often castigated by feminist theologians and medievalists for his diatribes against marriage and sexual passion— as well as for upholding virginity as the ultimate feminine ideal—I reveal him here as a character at war within himself, a man whose public persona and religious writing are in opposition to his private desires.

*

In several poems in this book, I refer to St. Jerome using his Greek name, Hieronymus *("devout"), during the earlier periods of his life.*

M.S.

The Father of Punctuation

It is a river of gold, a well-stocked library,
that a man acquires who possesses
Jerome and nothing else. - Erasmus

Father of Punctuation

In moments between preoccupations, in those pauses
punctured by the sound of malm being ground up
by bricklayers, or by the scolding magpies, or by

Paula praying quietly with her garnet beads—
the click and suspirations—he swabs his brow and
thinks about what sets apart one interval from another:

how a specific point must be molded into significance;
how each phase of an Idea must be syncopated, or
rotated, isolated or expanded, until its complexity

rings as clear as brook water enshrined in a chalice.
And so he devises a system of symbols to serve as
toggles and bridles, pulleys and beams, sutures, store

houses, stopgaps, funnels, fonts, ferrules, pipe joints,
flasks, flashing, stoups, basins, hinges, splines,
lids, signposts, road markers, chain links, spindles,

faucets, footbridges, ducts, channels and frets, braces,
gears, mauls and gavels, girders and girdles, brackets,
clasps and gridirons, tiepins, torques and tourniquets.

But he must strive to make his symbols swift
and supple, like swallows' wings, economical in
stroke, uniform in use, non-ornamental, plain.

The marginalia of his pages bespeak his toil,
littered with the dashed off tokens, teardrop
shapes, cryptographic crescents, quaint codes

and puzzling ciphers of his mind's hieroglyphic
quest for shapely marks, some which signal when
to stop, where to pause, how one thought unites

another, or how it subdivides itself, or multiplies
its meaning, or terminates a ponderous question.
It takes him years to divine this system which

neatly supersedes Greek's network. How precisely
he lays out the deft marks—solidus, hyphen and punctus,
a doubled virgula suspensiva, ampersand, subscript,

vinculum, ivy-leafed hedera, parentheses, and last—
the philosophical, obscure economy of the ellipses.
He looks up from his fine labors: the night sky

blackly mirrors back to him the roiling galaxy
of quaking stars, fossil planets, the broadlit swath of
the Milky Way—all glowing ornaments of God's mind.

St. Jerome the Hermit

The chilly blood stands still around my heart. – Virgil

Self-banished to the Chalcis desert for three years,
Hieronymus delved deeply into his sacred texts,

sleeping little and eating less, lingering for hours
in the hush of dawn to recite a litany of vows,

to compose copious epistles to church elders,
and to purify his sunburned body until it shone

as a fitting, sacred temple for the Holy Spirit.
A student of Hebrew, Greek, Latin, Aramaic,

he became a bastion of knowledge, a stronghold
of biblical lore, his memory dazzling, his vast

commentary acute, but troubling to some of
his fellow clerics, whose messages from Rome

urged him to purge himself of so much learning,
idolatry of the intellect, too stringent an asceticism.

Sometimes he wearied of words. Sometimes
the world beckoned in wanton ways: summer's

exuberance warbled and trilled outside his door;
then lewd thoughts would singe his aims, encoiling

him in unchaste shows of yearning, his blood
scalding his veins, his body rigid and pulsing.

There were days of blowzy light, when he flinched
to hear the sultry voices of distant washerwomen;

when even the sound of burbling water stirred him,
or the sight of an earthworm's swollen clitellum—

when the deft, rhapsodic mating of damselflies
wholly undid him, brought him to a misery of

fidgeting, so that he had to plunge his hands into
brambles to punish them for kneading his groin.

Even his dreams tormented him with impure visions
of Ruth or Sarah, of Bathsheba purloining David's gaze

as she bathed, of the slow unveiling of her limbs,
the sleek anointing of her breasts, thighs, lips.

Spasms of anger seized him on waking, driving him
to orgies of prayer, or to shatter another wasp's nest

under his roof, so his face and arms would bear,
unshielded, the barbed attacks of swarming daggers.

But he grew stronger. He outmatched his longings
for flesh with his striving toward redemption—

remedying himself with a remoteness toward others,
housing himself in sanctity like a priest's reliquary,

where he could polish the sacred bones of his belief
into a wintry splendor, a brittleness beyond touch.

(Chalcis Desert, 375 C.E.)

A Celestial Salaam

Be like the grasshopper and make night musical...
Sing with the Spirit...

Too extreme, the austerities of the Eastern anchorites
Hieronymus met in the wilderness, those skeletal Syrians,
athletes of wisdom—but also illiterate and monolingual,

filthy, hirsute, grossly wrinkled from exposure, hunger.
One lived in a ground hole smaller than a fox's burrow.
Another survived forty days of Lent on fifteen dried figs.

One toothless man festooned himself with two hundred-
fifty pounds of iron chains; his neighbor protected himself
from distractions by living atop a column, praying alone.

Though admiring them, Hieronymus shunned their company,
preferring to keep his fasts and vigils in his spacious cave,
then welcoming visits from Evagrius, from brother monks

and the Christian convert, Barininas, his Hebrew tutor.
He set himself *to learn an alien alphabet and strove*
to pronounce the hissing, aspirate words. What labor!

How often he despaired! How often he gave up, only
to swear stubbornly again that he would master it.
And so he did. Sequestered as a hermit cloaked in

his separate darkness, his faith became an arabesque
embossed upon his tongue, his mind gilt by a map of glory,
and the mystical emptiness of the desert stilled his pulse.

He slept on bare earth, drank only water, spurned meat.
He groaned, wept, prayed all the more vigorously when
harrowed by guilty memories of his youth's *sweet fires*

of sensual pleasure, and he thought often of castration.
He commanded his body to be as stone, deadened, so
he could free his soul to ascend and soar with angels.

One night ecstasy seized him and he felt his body lift
and rise slowly above its own floored shadow— Heaved
into rapture, he felt like crowing to the stars, exploding

into confetti as the moon washed his floating form in
its milky lather—he broke then into blissful laughter, air-
borne by the Spirit, as he sailed across the infinite sands.

(Syria, 377 C.E.)

At the Country Estate of Evagrius

...about the middle of Lent, a deep-seated fever fell upon my weakened body, and while it destroyed my rest completely—the story seems hardly credible—it so wasted my unhappy frame that scarcely anything was left of me but skin and bone. Meantime, preparations for my funeral went on; my body grew gradually colder, and the warmth of life lingered only in my throbbing breast. Suddenly I was caught up in the spirit and dragged before the judgment seat of the Judge; and here the light was so bright, and those who stood around were so radiant, that I cast myself upon the ground and did not dare look up. Asked who and what I was, I replied: "I am a Christian." But He who presided said: "Thou liest, thou art a follower of Cicero and not of Christ. For 'where thy treasure is, there will thy heart be also.'" Instantly I became dumb, and amid the strokes of the lash—for He had ordered me to be scourged—I was tortured more severely still by the fire of conscience, considering with myself that verse, "In the grave who shall give thee thanks?" Yet for all that I began to cry and bewail myself, saying: "Have mercy upon me, O Lord: have mercy upon me." - Letter XXII

*

I returned to the upper world, and to the surprise of all, I opened eyes so drenched with tears that my distress served to convince even the incredulous. And that this was no sleep nor idle dream, such as those by which we are often mocked, I call to witness the tribunal before which I lay, and the terrible judgment which I feared. May it never, hereafter, be my lot to fall under such an inquisition! I profess that my shoulders were black and blue, that I felt the bruises long after I awoke from my sleep, and that henceforth I read the books of God with a zeal greater than I had previously given to the books of men. - XXII

(Antioch, 375 C.E.)

The Vision

For days now, Evagrius has abandoned his multitude of tasks
to tend to Hieronymus's fevers, the elder priest's tinctures of
belladonna and juniper helpless against the visitor's delirium.

Dimly through his illness, Hieronymus hears: slowed cadences
of tillers' songs; then a cacophony of street urchins carping;
the stabbing voices of ibis or whooping cranes from far fields.

From open windows, these sounds enter and convulse in his ears,
becoming catalysts for recovery, though he knows he is dying.
Vectors of fear climb his backbone, tamp his veins with ice.

One morning he hallucinates so vividly he believes he has
passed into limbo's shadowed world, until he sees a centipede
shimmy up the plaster wall his cheek rests against, and he gasps,

recognizing it as the devil's mascot, a small, glittering thing,
shovel-headed and deadly, poised to sting his sore-encrusted lips.
Then he falls into a solid slumber, sleeping numbly for days.

Hieronymus awakens into midnight's stasis to find himself
transported to a heavenly tribunal, its grounds composed of
slabbed gold, its sky so refulgent it momentarily blinds him.

God sits on a throne surrounded by angels astride tigers.
His face gleams, a cloud of ignited molecules that endlessly
float, collide, vibrate, shimmer, and rejoin each other's light.

God bellows at him, his voice ear shattering, earth-splitting.
Yes, it's true: three archangels brutally lash his back with spines
cut from sickle weed, cactus, pampas grass, and sword bush;

yes, yes, Hieronymus falls to his knees, begs for divine mercy—
and yes, he weeps copious tears of contrition, begs for deliverance
from God's wrath—and yes, he dismembers his mortal conscience,

vowing never again to consort with pagan authors like Cicero—
But such is the stubborn nature of secrecy and shame that never
will the priest reveal in his life's voluminous letters and treatises

his *failure* to confess his foremost sins before God, his failure
to excrete the sludge clogging his heart, and to admit what most
defrocks his causes, emasculates his resolve: his utter slavery to

passion, his addiction to the *eudaimonia* of flesh, and to the high
voltage of ambition, that enslaver of reason and faith's despoiler.
He endures the whiplashings. He awakens into a new despair.

(Antioch, 374 C.E.)

St. Jerome's Dreams (I)

Beneath the Jerusalem cross he sleeps soundly.
Extinguished like the day, his tallow candle; his scrolls
closed and silent; his field of vision retracted inward.

His floor-anchored mat's infested with lice, yet
he no longer wakes to pinch and plunder them;
his suffering's so minuscule, private, it's an opiate.

Operose days, obverted nights. He exhales deeply,
And soon the dreams. There's nothing he can do but
surrender wholly to them, though they undo him.

Tonight he dreams himself wandering a somber land.
Thick grapevines clamber over a dead orchard's wall;
renegade red ants bespeckle the ground like cinders.

A young woman clad in ragged stoles stands alone
at a crossroads before him, her left eye blackened.
Her breasts are uncovered, ruddy as crab apples.

He stares, thinking—dream-tranced, immobile—
that she must be the genius loci, a tender of fruit,
or else a manifestation of Tamar, bruised by Amnon.

He steps closer, sees her teeth are chattering,
her feet clad in thorns, her lips blood-smeared,
her neck's sinews drawn tight like warriors' bows.

He would like to sink, to plunge far down into earth
to escape her grim stare, her female pathos, but
he feels joined to her, as if by parabiosis, or by

some fluke of destiny that would cruelly wed
a holy man, a celibate, to this battered apostate,
this libidinous chimera, or worse, to the devil.

He reels away from her, nauseated, recoiling,
but she reaches out, pulling him to her breasts
with a flinching force, pushing him to his knees.

Suckle me, she commands as, gagging, his mouth
opens, his lips fastening on the engorged areola,
the nipple smoldering against his dry tongue.

Suddenly he is ravenous, and her milk gushes
down his parched throat to his stomach, where
it then radiates through his intestines, limbs,

through his arteries and veins, coursing a radiance
everywhere, until every fiber and cell's illuminated,
singing, vibrating with light, with terrible joy.

He awakens with a jolt, his erection so taut that
it throbs achingly, like a glutted, excised heart.
Tremblingly he draws his long, jagged fingernails

across his chest, tearing the older, healed scabs
and scars into new crosshatchings of lines,
blood-matted, oozing. He rises, gathers the salt.

(Chalcis Desert, 377 C.E.)

The Miracle

Fainting dazes for two weeks: he's suffered his severest fast;
his stomach's shrunken down to the size of a child's fist—
he feels skeletal, lighter than a willow leaf, almost vaporous—

His once porcelain teeth have turned a mottled gray; his nails
look like graphite; the skin on his hands grows loose, flaccid;
his eyes go blank, his mind hemmed in, paralyzed by prayer.

And amid the dense urban crowds thronging Rome's streets,
the mass of human commotion stirring or stifling all quarters,
Hieronymus feels world-imperiled, alone, spiritually gutted.

So, through a gate in the Aurelian Wall, along the Via Appia,
then down again into the catacombs he wanders this holy day
to pay silent tribute to St. Sebastian's arrow-pierced bones,

and to find the tombs of Paul, Jewish missionary from Tarsus,
and Simon Peter, fisherman from Bethsaida in Galilee, both
saints condemned to death by Nero. Hieronymus stops before

their vaults, for something flickers beyond his oil lamp, behind
the wall inscribed with sacred graffiti, near a frieze of the Passion:
faintly, a feathery oscillation, and then an embryonic orb of gold

begins growing upward from the room's arched, dim corner,
and air rushes around the priest in invisible fountains spurting
and spewing iridescence—He sees now, *yes*, he *sees* them—

alabaster shoals emerging from a rotating geometry of light:
flocks of angels unweaving themselves in glowing filaments
from basalt tombs, and unruly rows of cherubim gliding along

dazzling diagonals of eerie beacons— His head, a glass cupola,
fills with a rain of diamonds: everywhere the soft machines of
rising seraphim, a bewildering profusion of wings, their silver-

foiled sleeves opening outward to him, their lyrical bell-voices
igniting a bonfire of astral flames—He sees archangels descend,
arise, all haloed by brilliant sunbursts, their molten diadems

regaling their heads, their beautiful faces lit by an extravagant
suffusion of love—then, a hailstorm of glittering mica swirls
a shower of sparks around him, shards of churning, lit ions—

holy *Virgin*!—she floats in mid-air before him—and a fragrance
now of gardenia, jasmine, of hyacinth and lavender permeates
the stale air...Then *darkness* envelops him: darkness absolute,

profound, irrevocable, abject, solid; a terrible, blinding darkness.
In that vacuum, Hieronymus suddenly hears the wet plip-plop
of dripping water echoing and rebounding in booming implosions

of spiraling sound—and he feels his own heartbeat knocking
loudly in answer. He is not, will never be, alone. An endless
array of invisible marvels surrounds him. Elbowed by ghosts,

paused among the dead's bones, Hieronymus enters Eternity
through the threshold of his want. Hereafter, he'll divine
no mystery greater than his own enduring faith.

(Rome, 382 C.E.)

St. Jerome among the Widows

And so he gathered them about him like lost lambs,
the grief-assailed women, their voices surging

into prayer, their robes billowing with hosannas—
"Save us," they chanted, their profiles aglitter

with hope's bright tears, their aristocratic faces
ablaze with the fine lotus light of heaven.

Even after he'd received his holy orders, taken
his vows, he moved among an imperial crowd,

with its doughy dowagers and diplomats' widows,
women who, disaffected, often lurched from

one credo to another, ever searching the schist
of belief for a few hard granules of gold.

But there stood one among them, shadow-hooded,
who spun his heart like a kite: a Roman matriarch

named Paula, whose regal beauty intensified with
the extremity of her grief. He watched her closely.

Thinned by mourning, delicate and fervent,
she wavered on the periphery of his solemn gaze;

like a dragonfly she flitted from hymnal to altar,
her pale, oval face impervious to distraction,

her lips, pomegranate red, slightly puckering
around the liturgy's vowels and consonants.

She asked for nothing from him, unlike others,
who brazenly flirted with Hieronymus in the street,

who wore diaphanous gowns and bent low before
him, so he might glimpse their full, dun breasts.

Paula remained aloof, private, rarely speaking
to him and quickly disappearing after services.

For months he secretly studied her avid practice
of religious rites, seeing how slowly, slowly faith

lifted her from sorrow's miasma of doubt into
a radiant devotion spun from God's jubilation.

Never had he seen instilled in a woman such
pure piety and love. Her quiet, graceful motions

disturbed him, though, and nightly, sleeping alone
in his cell, he dreamed of her purifying ablutions—

as if stationed behind her bathing screen, hidden
from Paula's view, he witnessed an intimate ritual:

saw how she slipped her robes down her torso,
so they puddled around her narrow feet; saw

her maid undrape voile stoles from her shoulders,
so she could step naked into the sunken, marble bath,

her thighs slightly rippling the azure waters
as she sunk down to immerse her whole body;

he saw how her brown breasts shivered tautly
as her maid poured rivulets down her lithe nape;

he watched with wonder as she lay back against
her silken pillow, allowing herself to float upward

to the water's surface, her round belly burnished,
her swatch of pubic hair glistening like obsidian.

In the dream—the same dream drowning his senses
nightly—she arose from her bath slowly to be

toweled dry by her maid, who then anointed her
arms and legs, her supple back, smoothing

scented oil into the hollows and sleek planes
of her plush skin—slick and pliant, flushed

by heat and friction—until she shimmered from
every pore, aglow like an unearthly Helen.

When he awakened, he felt scoured, his spirit
drained, his mind destitute, his faith gouged out.

It was always midnight then, the monastery
still as death, scant moonlight drizzling his cot.

His body still shuddered under the dream's grip,
and he cursed Eve's treachery, despising all women

for enslaving men to lust, and hating himself
most for his abiding hunger for forbidden gifts.

He would whip and lash himself ruthlessly then,
scoring his body with ridged seams, red stripes

flayed open and re-torn into awful ribboned ruts.
One night, exhausted, his palms slick with blood,

he swore an oath to God: tomorrow he'd advise
the widows on the virtues of going without baths.

(Rome, 383 C.E.)

St. Jerome's Dreams (II)

It was the night following Paula's departure
for the coast—she missed Eusto's company—

when he was hurtled again into a nightmare,
one clothed deceptively in the pearlescent hues

of an unfolding dawn: he stood in lush meadows
stippled vividly with bright periwinkles opening;

tendrils of new growth fawned his feet, and
a squall of star anise and daisies drew his eyes

across the blooming pastures of rampant spring.
He leaned against an aromatic balm of Gilead,

its evergreen needles musty, damp with dew,
and his lungs swelled with a verdant serenity.

And then they came: a band of naked maidens
slipped down from its branches, encircling him,

their hands clasped, their long hair loose, unruly—
strung with cornflowers and cockleshells—

their roseate breasts firm as gourds, crowned
with pebble-taut nipples, their varicolored pubes

thrusting inward toward him as the women
danced in circles dizzyingly, their laughter

orchestral and defiant, their mouths open—
oh the torment of their flushed, distended lips—

their voluptuous bodies swaying in serpentine
motions, their smooth bellies grazing him as

they closed in, and their humid breath washing
over him in waves of cinnamon and clove;

then one virgin pulled him toward her,
while another cupped her slender hands

around his genitals, unfastened his surplice,
coaxed his member into her velvet mouth,

as another maiden, behind him, wrapped her
olive arms around his neck to press her sun-

warmed breasts into the muscles of his back—
while the others moaned and undulated like sea

creatures roused by watery currents of rife
desire; and he was falling, sliding down,

down into their soft, slithering bodies, swept
into a roiling mass of female flesh, his face

nuzzling the moist nest of a maiden's crotch,
his penis poised like a spear above two thighs,

which opened inwards to unpursed petals: now
widening, welcoming, flushed purple, pulsating—

And he awoke, drenched in sweat, and began
to strum and pummel his sex that thrust

its club upwards, clawing his skin raw, while
the coterie of wanton women still writhed

transparently upon him, bringing him now to
the edge of madness, until at last he broke

open, his seed spilling in throbs on his groin.
Spent, he lifted the crucifix from his neck

and jabbed it into his brow, stabbing it
over and over into his sin; then he cast it

across the room to pick up the heavy stone
he used as a pillow, wielding blow after

hard blow into his chest, unstifling his sobs,
bludgeoning himself, bruising his ribs,

bashing his shoulders, stomach, his calves,
until his body was studded, stunned by pain.

When, several mornings later, Paula returned
alone to Jerome's hermitage, her heart stopped

to see the holy man's wound-tormented body.
He would not speak to her for forty days.

(Bethlehem, 386 C.E.)

Bethlehem

They labor side-by-side, reworking Ecclesiastes,
Paula sometimes vexed by Jerome's inferior Greek,
though she praises his diligent metamorphosis,
his growing "spiritual manhood," a phrase which,

when he says it, reddens her cheeks. As always,
they toil to revitalize the old Latin versions, replace
the Hebrew omissions, winnow out redundancies
and musty renditions of their sacred Scriptures.

Despite the first sudden rainfall of the season,
a horned owl perches above the sodden eaves,
hooting mildly; its distracting notes remind him
now of the proverb: *The ass listened to the lyre,*

the pig to the trumpet. They listen to the Spirit,
translating through the night, avoiding any
adultery of the tongue (that affected lisp some
Romans adopt to belie their country breeding).

As dawn enters his room, Paula bows to prayer.
She has thinned to a transparency of herself,
and he sees that her sackcloth is ragged but clean.
Her piety's unrivalled; her womb's turned golden.

Together they shun the hearth, endure the cold that
seeps into their fingers. Though he sates his hunger
with the cherries Eustochium sent, Paula fasts
again, bending close to read her threadbare missal.

What honey is sweeter than to know God's wisdom?
Our riches are to meditate in the law of our Lord
day and night, to knock at the closed door,
to receive the "three loaves of the Trinity,"

and, when the Lord goes before us,
to walk upon the water of the world.

(October 387 C.E.)

A Nocturne

"Uneven numbers are the joy of God." – Virgil

A cobalt night and the eager, stark tutelage of the stars.
He sees the Centaur drawing his bow, hero of midnight hunters,

his equine haunches straining as if poised to charge
a pagan god's descent, his profile a twinkling diaglyphic.

After hourless days of study, the priest has wandered outside
to lower his cramped body into a hammock strung between palms.

He meditates on the centripetal force God works upon his mind,
what drives Jerome to an inner glossolalia, wherein scores of voices

vie to seize his tongue so that he'll speak what remains unspoken.
He must mold ten thousand sentences into crystalline alms,

despite the half-starved hunger that hollows, hallows his breast:
his famished yearning for more knowledge, his endless journey.

*

Beyond Jerome's monastery walls, Bethlehem sleeps, immune
to what fuels his thoughts, burns his brow as if with hot wax.

His addiction's more potent than Beelzebub's seductions,
for the Lord of the Flies now seems less than a dour mimic

of divine power, an inept artificer, a lowly, winged cockroach fit
only for gnawing away the world's false skins, his insect hands

wringing each other, his complex eyes grotesque and myopic—
To conquer evil, one must know how *not* to disappear

into the shadows of history. One must climb the steep ladders
of sacred scaffolding that uplift and reveal the Divine Laws—

*

But how does a man live outside his own time, remove himself
backward four hundred years into the past, to suddenly stand among

the others bowing before a crude, boxwood cradle? How can he
then contain his breathlessness, his heart-pounding, terrible shaking?

He sees the pig, the sheep, the ox, even the manger's grizzled dog,
encircling her as she lowers her breast to the newborn Child, a bronze

light siphoning down from the sky, a sound of flutes, lyres, a *cornu*
saturating the night air, a fragrance of saffron or sandalwood rising

from the straw to fill his nostrils as the shepherds and Magi form
a stunned crescent of bodies poised before that dazzling mystery—

*

Jerome shakes his head, trying to loosen the hold of the nativity
upon him— There are too many vanishing points in the mind,

too many provinces alluring him to their remote or spectral truths;
such bulletins from heaven may bring confusion, as well as clarity.

He aspires to an odd singularity, this prophet of holy alphabets,
pilgrim who labors until his fingers bleed, his eyes blinded to sleep.

Dawn approaches. He hears the outlaws on the far hill crying out
to their captors; he sees the sky turning milky as an angel's throat.

He will toil like the distant orange groves, each day being a tree
bearing glowing globes, each fruit bearing the sweetness of divinity.

(Bethlehem, 388 C.E.)

St. Jerome Rests from His Labors

He raises the stoneware amphora to his lips
and drinks deeply, red wine speckling his beard.

The Sabbath. A distant donkey's bray scolds him
momentarily, but he puts aside self-recriminations.

Fasting on water today isn't enough: wine rouses
his blood for the depthless hours of supplication.

Sobriety never abandons him, nor will his spine
straighten again like a sapling's: too many years

he's knelt by splay or vestibule, so many decades
of prayers, his bony knees harden like a camel's.

On the periphery of his mind, the woman sulks.
She's done her dawn ablutions, her stint of sweeping,

making bread: she's worked silently this Sabbath,
and now she's withdrawn into a corner to mend.

Why so sullen, he asks, but Paula's lips are closed.
Sultry drafts gust around the sanctum, stirring

the dust into small piles. She begins to weep.
Were she an anvil, he would strike her hard

with the mallet of his contempt; or if she hung,
like a dull bell, he would swing her clapper

into a deafening tumult of rebuke and echo.
But she bears a mortal stench, and seems softer

than an ash with her womanly sorrow—gray,
easily rent—and he feels ambushed by pity for her,

remembering the weary leagues of their pilgrimage,
the weeks surviving on mulch, fungi, wild ginger.

He can't banish nor rid himself of her, for she
festers like a disease in his entrails, a malady

that paradoxically quickens his pulse and stops
his heart—she's his stigma, a visible reprisal

for his fiercely suppressed, dream-borne yearnings:
he knows how lust quells or dwarfs noble ambitions,

so he returns once more to his sanctum, bitter,
violently thirsty for another swig of wine.

(Bethlehem, 394 C.E.)

Translation

His aims are not palliative, nor damned, nor
unruly—he knows this—they are pre-ordained
by God, for Jerome exists like a stonemason's tool,

solely to decipher and reveal what raw quartz or
travertine refract: those holy designs yet unlaunched
into form, as yet embryonic, unwitnessed, submerged.

He refuses to swerve, to serve any other call.
Hebrew syllables halter him both to this world
and to Eternity; they transport him, year after year,

to another firmament, to a light-entrellised place
where every sound supplies meaning with glory,
where God's mystery ignites every pore within him.

Sometimes Latin words flush gold from the ore,
robbing flares of music from the Hebraic strophes;
sometimes he coins new words, but always falteringly,

wanting to be silver-tongued, eloquent as David,
as wise as Solomon, as undaunted as daring Saul.
Yet the two dialects grow confounded in his mouth.

He's growing old. Arthritis cripples the knuckles
of his right hand, and he's forced now to bend low
over his scrolls, squinting, blinking away blind spots.

When the sun rises and day's domain unfurls anew
before him, his mind thrashes again with hope—poised
as he is between faith and purpose on death's fulcrum.

(Bethlehem, May 415 C.E.)

St. Jerome Alone

He wanders the graveyard stricken with loss.
The candelabrum he carries trails hot wax across

the flagstone steps he treads, burns his knuckles:
but he's oblivious, as usual, to pain's stratagems.

He hopes to find communion here, at her crypt,
to enrich his anguish, or assuage it, by straining

towards a strangeness which consumes him now
in her absence, steeping his life in bewilderment.

He was stupid with love for her, soiled and pricked
by unspoken affection, halved and quartered by her—

stung, flailed, roused, entangled, assailed over
and over again by her erudition, her stately grace,

by her silent forbearance, her womanly cheer,
by her softness—as if, particle by minute particle,

she arose from an embankment of clouds—and
by her devotion, so pure it rivaled the Virgin's.

Her grave is strewn with fresh laurel leaves,
with the detritus from straw wreaths, wild roses,

willow strands that scampering insects plunder.
He sets down the flickering candles to crouch

beside the planed surfaces of smooth marble,
to press his forehead against the cold tomb.

She was nothing and everything to him:
ardent follower, servant and sister, gleaner

of verses, a progenitor of propriety, noun
wed to his verbs, a grain of salt, speckle of

dew on the green blade of each rising day,
ghost, caulk of his lonely hours, companion.

She moved so gently through his world that
molecules of air were barely stirred to step

aside, and rivulets of wind dispersed to spend
their vanishing in a quiet abstraction of sighs.

He recalls her luminous, dreamy face, her
life forever hovering between two realms—

and he feels the stale air stir and quicken
with her mild electricity, as if she's begun

to occupy his flesh invisibly, as if her body
whirls on within him, as his own destiny.

(Bethlehem, January 30, 404 C.E.)

St Jerome's Casket

Flatter than the desert's horizon, his coffin,
rough hewn from olivewood, then bleached
in vinegar, dried and oiled with linseed balm.
It stands alone, installed in the dimmest corner
of his bare chapel, a single palm leaf laid gently
upon its middle, a simple cross adorning its prow.

Now the villagers come and gawk in mute pairs,
eyeing the austerity of his face, its mossy beard
as white as soapstone, his lips as parched in
death even as they were in life. A fanatic.
Something too holy in the calmly rigid hands,
in the smooth, unlined palms, tapered fingers.

Why had he lived so long among them, yet apart?
Why had bevies of doves perched on his tilting
rafters, winter after winter, as if awaiting his call?
Long he'd hovered on the outskirts of their minds
like a thunderstorm on the brink of breaking.
They felt no cheer or grief to see him stilled at last.

Black drapes. Dried willows. His last vessel
grafted with filaments of silvered cobwebs, dark
seeping slowly up into the room's distilled moments,
and only the clerical flies to drone hosannas.
If only he'd awaken and speak once more to them:
upbraid them for worshipping lesser gods.

(Bethlehem, circa 420 C.E.)

A Matriarch of Rome

Dum spiro spero—

A Matriarch of Rome

(July 383 C.E.)

A flinty afternoon stirred by a boost of breezes
brings back her other life—as distant now as the pouts
of her young daughters, as remote as the mercurial love
of her headstrong husband with his lapis amulets,
his stable of roan horses rippling with fervor...

Their days together rich, grandiose: cashmere shawls,
enameled flasks of sangria, strung emeralds crowding
her neck like beetles, marble walls and zebrawood tables,
the traffic of servants, raw fragrance of stacte, water's
clear slither, splash, and spill from myriad fountains.

She remembers their ebony bed's alcove, its criosphinx
mantle, the huge ram's head hewn from gray onyx;
she again stands by their window to gaze out on a city
scalded by summer gusts, the air thickened with grit
from the numismatists' shops, the nutmeg vendor
stalled under her eaves, hurtling oaths at a soldier.

All this, all this worldly commotion riots again
through her in painful explosions—a vision of Toxotius
stoking the coals, his muscled thighs auburn in firelight;
her palace herbarium fragrant with pressed petals;
taste of lichee and cherimoya, wisps of frangipani.

Winter nights she pored over her silver zodiac, plotted
her girls' betrothals by the stars' presage or turning.
In later years she was too often revived by passion—
the bloody spectacles at the coliseum, her yielding
to the intoxication of Remus's lips. Yes, it was true:
after Toxotius left her a widow, she coarsened.

Now the past's pageantry seems merely a paralysis
of will, or of faith, or both. Her life then, all idolatry,
indulgence, a plasma engulfing her in a brocade of sin.
All her protean wealth now nothing but dust and lint;
her husband, daughter—supine under the mimosa.

Eustochium and Blesilla

(Rome, June 378 C.E.)

For their birthdays—both being born like twin stars
on the same June's blue-moon dawn—their father
nuzzled them on his bulging lap, stroking their arms,
sable and slender, and gave them nephrite necklaces.

He delicately caught the clasps around their slim necks,
brushing aside the girls' black curls, long helixes as
silken as pheasant feathers, coiled and oiled for him.
Did the anger first stir in me then, on that day?

I watched how his chest heaved with a passion
unkempt and unbefitting a father, how his breath
went untamped by propriety, his heart making itself
a nuisance under his linen tunic. His brow sweating.

Eusto turned his large head in her fine hands
to kiss his mouth, while Blesilla pulled one earlobe
gently, calling him "meus Pater Deus." I thought:
They are civet cats, baby whores, fire-starters.

I thought: no minatory words or gazes—I must not
on their birthdays, must not chide him, nor them,
but quell my fury like a forger incusing a medallion
with quick hammer blows, steeping it, molten, in water.

Such was the decayed state of our city's customs,
that incest was excused among patriarchs, or,
at most, looked at askance, yet it went unpunished.
As our gods behaved, so we mortals mimicked them.

Oil lamps flickered on the mosaic table as he purred
like a lion, his daughters pleased, nervous, teasing
his eyelids with rose petals, Silla moistening her smile
as her buttocks rubbed against his crotch, and Eusto coy,

whispering naughty tidbits in his ear, or tickling him,
her nubile breasts romancing his chest, the small nipples
grazing his skin with goosebumps; his voice hoarse,
his eyes wild and clouded, aroused and tender, glittering.

I could not overcome the tincture of bitterness rising
like venom in my throat, the tightening in my womb; then,
strangely, I felt a geologic gorge in me cracking wide,
a deep cleft of hungry yearning splitting me open—

Paula's Circle

(Rome, 381-382 C.E.)

Evenings, we gather at Marcella's Aventine mansion.
Our hostess softly greets each of us: pigeon-toed Principia,
Asella with her lopsided wigs, mild-mannered Furia—

(oh irony inherent in her name)—lithe Lea, whose beauty
rivals Athena's, green-eyed Titiana with her guttural stutter,
and finally, large-boned Thea, whose Greek is meticulous.

We've eschewed the decadence of the feasting table,
renounced our lavish *stola*, our gold-embroidered *pallium*
used for encloaking ourselves like peacocks in silken veils;

we've removed diadem, earrings, bracelets, anklets, rings,
and put aside forever our lanolin creams, earthen rouges,
antimony mascara, our eyes' glittering hematite shades.

Among these barefaced ladies, I'm richly clothed in faith;
my shy-lipped daughters shimmer as my brightest rubies.
We pray together, sing Hebrew songs that Hieronymus

intones in his deep baritone, his beard's sable tip dipping
to punctuate the verses in a way that my Eustochium and
Blesilla find humorous—though they stifle their grins.

Beyond our circle, our friends revel in gluttony, strain
to appease the sexual greed consuming their bodies
with the speed of a straw fire, or drink themselves into

impotence and cruelty, mistreating their own children.
I, too, sailed those turbulent seas and nearly drowned.
But for this priest, I would have severed my life—

O how to describe the delicacy of my newborn love?
How to express this tumult of yearning, calmed only
by brushing my lips against a prayer's silent splendor?

Chastity becomes my refuge, my shelter: I enter its
shining white room—windows flung open to heaven—
and a shock of electric pulse blasts into my heart,

a field of anti-gravity moves through my body—
God's invisible hand— my naked spirit consumed,
my life dissolving into milk-cloud, atoms, dust—

Paula's Tale: Mourning

(January 382 C.E.)

In my thirty-third year, like our Savior,
  I was ripped apart by death, although I
myself did not die. A spring contagion seized
  my Silla's heart, bursting it asunder,

until nothing could bring her fitful
  laughter back; nothing could reverse
her quiescence, revivify her cold lips,
  nor rupture her lengthening silence.

I recalled the grinding of her teeth
  at night, her starling chatter over
breakfast, her noontime chiromancy
  lessons, her stable boy infatuations.

My Silla! How could you leave us
  here, still tracing your lovely profile
with warm hands, your marble bust
  incapable of outbursts or guile?

When you died, I thought the gods had
  grown even more cowardly than men;
I vowed to turn my back on them,
  to embrace only the tiny embers of joy

which illuminated your father's and
  sisters' faces, when weeks later I saw
how their eyes reflected a fierce ensnarement
  of love: your long-lashed, open-eyed measure.

In their gazes an eloquence of you still
  persisted, and this comforted me.
But, daughter, the gulfs of darkness only
  open into a more capacious darkness:

death is an emptiness spiraling into us
  like a drill, hollowing us out—deeper
and deeper—until the winds of loss
  shriek through us as through a tunnel.

Your father died. Do you know?
Our artisans had barely finished
carving the daffodils—your favorites—
to deck your tomb, when he, too,

succumbed to a fever, still swooning
with grief, and wildly frantic,
knowing that death stood by his bed-
side, an invisible sentry. He died

that same night, clutching your ribbons,
holding my gaze tormentedly.
I lurched from him blindly—for
I couldn't comprehend pain's roar

blasting my body, how my wracked flesh
storehoused its tremors, its terrors,
even though my mind veered and pitched
in a ruined stupor, numbed through

by death's narcosis, by its doubled blows.
Silla, see how two of your sisters
stir wands of incense around your altars,
how they cry out in their sleep, so

fearful that they'll join you and Papa,
or that I will leave them, too.
Our days slouch and rebound from
the tedium of our old habits.

Nothing replaces your touch or voice.
Your father's stallions grow restless.
Who will harness them now? Who
will tease music from his lyre?

Who will daub ointment on your wounds?
Little salamander, moss stoppers your ears.

The Spiral Pilgrimage

(Rome, October 382 C.E.)

I mill around.
I spill my thoughts.
I spool them up again.

I dream of wheelbarrows
bearing pyramids
of entrails.

I set fires:
to the damask curtains,
to locks of Silla's hair.

I cannot eat—
I scald my hands,
uproot the garden.

A dead mouse
paralyzes my will.
I shred my veils,

and collect aphids
in a broken conch.
I bury want.

I retch on emptiness,
sadness my
sanctum sanctorum.

How to go on?
How not to?
I could drown,

am drowning,
drenched in dross.
Or is this drought?

I'm lost: a zero
minus its circumference.
My thoughts zigzag

back and forth
from this void to
the one beyond.

I am lost, lost—
barely a gloss
on sorrow's map.

Remus

(Rome, December 382 C.E.)

Much as I want, need to abandon him,
I cannot. As flowering vines overwhelm
and consume a building's architectural façade,
so desire flows over my body, obscuring my will.

Even as he steps into the secret doorway
of my chamber, I feel my instincts thwarted,
violently overtaken by a calamity of cravings.
His body is a magnet, a spool, gravity itself.

After our frenetic couplings, a primal serenity
seeps into me, a euphoria of forgetfulness—
my husband's, daughter's voices evaporating
into the furthest recesses of my emptied heart.

And knowing that I desecrate my lover's
marriage vows causes me pain, despite
Remus's angry claim that his wife deprives him,
that her barrenness has riven their bonds.

So I seek the balm of tenderness within
his arms, am flattered by the legion captain's
gifts: a sparrow hawk contained in an ivory cage,
a Greek vase emblazoned with a vigorous Eros

pursuing a long-legged Psyche, her calm face
turned to the viewer with a seductive smile.
I treasure most the medallion that once hung
heavily from the nobleman's neck, a serpent

entwined in the horns of a rampaging bull—
signs of earthly power, a symmetry of control.
Soon enough I'll spurn his eager kisses and
those wildfires of my flesh that scald away,

layer by layer, the bitter trappings of my grief.
One final night, then: his succulent lips poised
over my breast, his enflamed body hovering
above me, and my soul yielding, yielding...

After Their Deaths

(Rome, April 383 C.E.)

Tendrils of sweet pea and morning glory cling tightly
to the outer courtyard balustrade, and as I climb,
I gaze down upon pink fuchsias the legion's captain
brought as an exotic offering for the new year.

The air is balmy with spring. The sky's belly
stretches over my head in a blue band stippled
with puce clouds; a rainbow stationed in the east
slowly dissolves above the acacia in the atrium.

I've returned from that lackluster altar at which
some friends scoff, thinking me a foolish woman
for becoming a Christian, for worshipping a man,
a Jew, no less, whose arms were pinioned, nailed

crudely to splintered wood, his red, ruptured hands
outstretched in martyrdom for his fickle brethren.
How can I tell these women about the long shiver
of awe that takes sanctuary within my bones?

How can I translate this reverence for God
from blasphemy, confusion, paradox, and doubt?
It saves me, even as it bruises me with longing.
They think my mourning's taken a dangerous turn:

and, yes, I held a brown asp to my bare throat,
begging it to puncture my jugular, to sever
my stunned days of endless weeping and drinking,
to blanch my mind of my girl's sweet, lost face.

I wear my sorrow like a veil, a caul of frost—
but it doesn't blind me: instead, it clarifies.
There are precise boundaries I can never cross,
I know this, and yet, I'm no longer myself.

Weeks ago, when Remus arose to tie the trusses
of his sandals, being still drowsy and drunk,
his skin smelling of sweetgrass, his groin sticky—
I'd grouse about his leaving me for his wife.

Now I can't tolerate his touch, his token leer
as he watches me from afar: I've closed my door.
That kind of passion only trammels the spirit.
I want a spare life, bare and Spartan, empty.

I grow more and more imperfect. I seethe.
These nights alone, I rub myself roughly with
tear-doused fingertips, or with my crucifix.
I am beyond grief. Each dawn my palms bleed.

Hieronymus and the Lion

(Rome, January 385 C.E.)

Legends grow slowly and askant the truth:
time confounds them or entwines their heroes
like vines so that they'll bear a single flower.

The slave Androcles, spared in the arena
by the lion who remembered his kindness,
for instance, served as the hero for a story

which I witnessed first, in an earlier year,
when Hieronymus and I traveled north
from Rome to secure some sacred texts.

We traversed an open field surrounded
by forests, and paused for lunch. I watched
a caterpillar crawl comically up a stick, as

suddenly a lion burst into our midst, its
fangs bared, its tail lashing: it crouched
before us growling, sinking on its hind legs,

snarling, while we sat stupefied by fear.
Seeing we didn't move to strike him, the lion
relaxed his shoulders, lowered his large head

to lick a suppurated forepaw, his tongue
gently lapping putrid flesh, where a thorn
protruded between clenched, clotted toes.

Arced over us, a copper sky, curiously silent.
I held my breath, feeling my heart tighten
to a burl, my bowels churning, astir with bile.

My teacher stood then, speaking softly, as
he neared the beast who watched the man's
approach with veiled lids and glinting eyes.

Hieronymus crouched down slowly, and with
a mother's tenderness, plucked out the thorn,
offering it on his open palm, to calm the lion.

With bulky dignity, the creature sighed, raised
his massive muzzle and dragged his great tongue
across my mentor's grizzled head, a loud purr

rumbling the air, vibrating the ground until
a clamor of termites erupted from it, dazed
by that lush, trembling noise, that deep engine.

Nights when I'm wild with strife, when love
seems as distant as a starless abyss, when
my teacher encloses himself in a bitter solitude,

I remember that intimate kindness, his gentle
touch upon the lion's paw, how courage wells
up at unforeseen moments and blesses us all.

The Yea Sayer

(Cairo, en route to Palestine, 385-386 C.E.)

I repair sere codices and tattered bodices:
I seem to have an affinity for mediating
between the sacred and the profane.

I accept my lot, trudging from marketplace
to liturgy, from wheelbarrow to stylus—
mending our clothes, tending the soul's fuel.

Today, the road's gravel is dimpled here
and there with mint, thumbnail bracts of dill.
Spring again, and the world's too lambent,

the distant fields ashiver with rain's varnish,
the dawn sky streaked with arterial blues
and violets, songbirds accenting the quiet.

I've embraced this life as would a ghost.
I grow old in my solitude, my thick hair
cropped, my ampullae emptied of perfume.

In the market, the women close their faces
to me: I'm served last, after the lepers, given
shrunken loaves, wormy dates, rancid oil.

Some spit behind me as I turn to leave,
or fling pebbles at my back—hard enough
to pepper my skin with stinging welts.

As usual, I take the least trod path back
to our austere hermitage, the longest way
emptied of travelers, but for misled goats,

or bony stray dogs keeping my company,
escorting me past the steadfast cypress,
lying wordlessly at my feet where I rest.

Today, two of them mate crookedly under
a casuarina tree, the female's wry face
a cameo of pain and heat, the male's penis

jamming into her like a fiery red pestle,
a froth oozing from where they're joined,
his fangs bared, his grunts almost rapturous.

I've vowed to leave the flesh's savors far
behind me, have salved my cravings with denial
and prayers, a fervid pledge of abstinence.

And still this crude spectacle of fornication
quickens me, plants an oily tension in my
thighs, clamps hot tongs about my groin,

until I'm drawing back the folds of my robe,
thrusting my hand down to rub myself and
imagining that it's *his* body's flesh grazing

mine, *his* loins entwined around mine,
his mouth sucking my lips, *his* tongue's
soft wand tenderly wetting my mouth—

and I am falling, floundering, pitched,
fused to a spasm of release—O loneliness!
O arctic world! There is nowhere to go,

nowhere beyond the senses, for sanctity's
merely a mirage that vanishes with flesh.
The dogs stand stiffly now, buttocks joined,

one's face turned east, the other westerly:
both spent, yet welded together as one beast.
I whore myself to Eros, hoard my grief.

Obiter Dictum

(Bethlehem, 392 C.E.)

He sees me merely as part of the world's calligraphy
trapped in space: I'm just an apostrophe to him,
as inconsequential as a bone discarded by a stray,
as brief and unfixed as a spasm of lightning.

All *things* are equal to him: thorn bush and wasp,
wheel spokes, braided hemp, jug and knife, the dirt.
He drags his body through his days like a sack
filled with useless organs, bothersome needs,

stale urges which he's loath to meet, being mind-
cast far from the deliberations of flesh, from self.
Years ago I starved myself for him, anointed
my limbs with mustard oil and myrrh, bathed

my words in holy water, steeped my feral desires
in lime and terror, schooled my mind in saints:
a time when I lashed myself with briars, and slept
naked in a cave, where only bats heard my prayers.

I'm an ascetic to him, not a scholar, although
I, too, plow the white fields, plant seeds, reap
a great bounty from those verses he translates.
My presence holds no volume for him, no odor,

no vibration of sound, no scale nor weight.
I'm bland as chalk, ephemeral as a dust cloud.
But my heart beats on flamboyantly; my lips
may crack and bleed, but they still sweeten air.

I'm like a sphere of amber, a life distilled
within a life: a spider caught in ambient sap.
I turn to wild nature now, a disciple of grass:
slowly I'm learning the raindrop's gospel.

The Naysayer

(En route to Palestine, 386 C.E.)

Her fingernails skim the chill
from her cheek: a hushed scrim of gossip
echoes in her ears. *What they say.*
What they all *say*—that she is too mortal,
lost in a vast firmament of sin, that his shuffle
bespeaks a blight on his soul; his shadow
a black paradigm stirred by dust devils.

Mother of God, she mutters,
Why shouldn't our mock orange tree smell
fragrant, despite the dung bronzing its roots?
When strangers skirt their chapel, they round
the well to spit down its blue depths,
clearly smitten with malice,
their edgy gazes cold as dead planets.

She mends her loneliness with psalms.
His mind, so burred and blurred by Hebrew reveries,
can't know how tossed and bruised her heart is,
nor see the local boys, hidden by boulders, who
slyly await her baths, hoping to glimpse her breasts—
an ache piercing their groins, a fetid orchid
stanching their throats like a rancid host.

Though she's been tethered to his faith for years,
her riotous fevers of doubt persist: a plague
of misgivings buzzes around her, winged maggots.
What is eternal, she muses, *is loss.*
Grief, the compost for our love of God.
Her hands grow more and more remote to her.
She dreams of figs drenched in honey.

St. Paula among the Marigolds

(Bethlehem, 399 C.E.)

She's forsworn being a daughter, wife, widow, and mother,
savoring her roles as Christ's bride, servant to the poor—
Now, within the matrix of her convent, Paula enjoys the solace
of celestial stirrings, as she moves in orbit among chaste sisters,

those numinous, meek creatures who drift along the corridors
like thistledown—whose silences signal a silken renunciation.
Their hymns' sweet notes ring in her ears, syncopating time;
so, her months and years pass, a parade of spiritual devotions.

One morning, as she weeds the convent garden, she looks up
to see a sky of *cirrus uncinus*—a backdrop of mares' tails
spun from delicate white filaments, curling into hooks, tufts—
and suddenly, mid-breath, she feels Christ's touch upon her

brow and an abundance of grace expands her lungs until
she gasps, seeing shimmering before her a dark-eyed man
smiling down at her crouched form, his body so translucent
that the clouds radiating behind him permeate his fluid form—

He floats before her in empty air and she is poised in rapt
amazement—O stunned, O dazzled, O glorious reward—
O watcher—now look—be open-eyed—be undiminished,
for joy, joy! trumpets through her veins—blows her open—

Before Her Death

"So many of my songs are gone from me,
and even my very voice has left me now." – Virgil

Yearly, the slug crisscrosses his own tearstains,
the queen bee encrypts her hive with secret chambers,
the locust grafts his song upon fleeing shadows,
the worm weans herself on wolfbane, on stardust.

I sit in the heat of my own discontent, where
only the gruff sound of his voice replenishes me.
It is never enough to love, simply to love.
Better to cleave to the silver blade, its quiver.

Better to gather a basket of roses and lilies,
ivory and purple, to fast with strangers,
to bask in the body's hungers as in sunlight.
I bear witness to myself with meditation;

as one substratum of my heart calcifies,
another layer pleasures itself with memory:
my touch a chink in his armor, his touch
frugal, but scalding, and his gaze plainsong.

I grow hoarse. My virgins pile a pyramid of
fruits before me, to tempt me again to break
my fasting. I will not. Faith is episodic
initially—but these long years it's yielded

to something else…something slowly fluid—
a liberation of the senses, an animal wisdom.
I watch my sparrow granddaughter polish the pyx,
the nape of her neck softened by cilia of down,

her open face so like my own a lifetime ago—
contemplative as well water, a rosy cameo.
Is she suited for a nun's habit? I think perhaps
her fingers are better fitted to a cithera's strings.

Yet I find such flexibility of thought in her,
and an undefiled purity that enthralls me.
Little Paula, come sit on my wrinkled knees—
teach me to be like an angel struck dumb—

(Bethlehem, Summer 403)

The Labyrinth

(Bethlehem, January 25, 404 C.E.)

Death amazes me.
Hourly it changes its face, its disguises.
At dusk it was tentacular, a huge octopus
suspended over me, its elongated arms
writhing around my body, as if
to engulf me in sea slime.

At dawn, death knocked again
softly against my eyes' closed shutters.
This time it stood beside my couch—
a hermaphrodite—smiling, slowly waving
a palmyra fan to cool my hot skin.
I suppose that the poor, sutured creature
embodied the treason of flesh,
how entangled the sexes are,
but I felt soothed by the swoosh
of air, by death's tender ministrations.

Transformed again, death returned
at noon to inhabit Toxotius' young mien—
all hard muscle and beckoning lips—
in one hand, he offered me a carrier pigeon;
he held a bunch of grapes in the other.
I reached out to touch him, but his image
crumbled like ancient parchment.

A crepuscular sky brings death now:
I'm wandering through a long, thick maze
of geometric walls, their stones dry-stacked,
mildewed; I follow their pathways slowly,
arduously to reach whatever awaits me
at their center. My heart jitters.
What will confront me there?
My breast palpitates so wildly that
I can barely take these final steps
Leading me to my fate.

At its center, the maze's treasure:
a turbulence like shining mirrors catapults
brilliant light into a blinding radiance.
Rainbowed fragments beam outwards
from the blazing source:
our Lord and Savior stands alone,
garbed in sheets of shimmering sunlight.
I am absorbed into his golden aura,
as if lifted from gravity to his orbit—
his body a cathedral of lucent glass,
a diamond opening...

but I am being shaken now, and unfasten
my eyes to find my master weeping beside me,
great sobs heaving his chest, his rough hands
gripping my shoulders as if to pull me
back to the world, his scant prayers
evaporating into smoke, his face,
his touch, dissolving...

The Lost Diaries

In girum imus nocte et consumimur igni.

In circles we go in the night
and are consumed by fire.

Excerpts: Letters from Bethlehem

"Nothing human is alien to me." – Terence

"In the old days, even Jerusalem went a-whoring and opened her feet to everyone that passed by." – Ezekiel, xvi.25
- Letter LXXXIV

*

What trouble and expense it cost me to get Baraninas to teach me under cover of night. For by his fear of the Jews, he presented to me in his own person a second edition of Nicodemus.
- Letter LXXIX

*

Do we not see numbers of heathens, Jews, heretics, and men of various opinions rolling in the mire of lust, bathed in blood, surpassing wolves in ferocity and kites in rapacity, and for all this, the plague does not come nigh their dwellings?
- Letter LXVIII

*

Death came through Eve, but life has come through Mary.
- Letter XXII

The Lost Diaries

Prologue

After that pious master, my father, Eusebius,
sent me off (despite my mother's wails)
to distant Rome, I became first a scholar, then
an orator, and, finally, a man of the world.

I lived in a dormitory for boys, all of us tutored
by Aelius Donatus, a maestro of grammar;
I spent my adolescence studying great rhetoric
with the eloquent harelip, Victorinus.

Hour after hour, I breathed in Virgil and Cicero,
Sallust, Terrence, Plautus, and Horace,
or I argued over my first Greek renderings
with my beloved, sharp-tongued Rufinus.

On Sundays my friends and I often toured
the tombs of the apostles and martyrs.
We entered crypts dug out of earth's depths
which, along walls on the passage's sides,

entomb the bodies of buried men and women.
They were so dark it seemed the prophecy
of the Psalmist was fulfilled: "Let them go
down alive into hell." *Only here and there*

did a ray of light penetrate from above and
relieve the horror of that blackness.
Then we'd grope back through the darkness,
remembering Virgil's line: "Everywhere

dread grips my heart; even the silence
frightens me." Thereafter, when I emerged
into blinding sunlight, the world appeared
irreversibly altered. Shadows deepened.

Death entered my dreams then—long weeks
I'd awaken from night terrors seizing me
by the throat, pummeling my nerves; death
lurking like a poison in my dry mouth—

So I began keeping these secret diaries, if only
to tame the demon that taunted me daily,
to know its masks, its pulse, its dark habits,
that I might banish it from my thoughts.

No one, not even Rufinus, knew of them, for
I hid my confessions under a loose stone
beneath my bed, where only occasional earwigs
danced over my sins, over my nightmares.

*

For sixty years I've hauled my diaries with me,
a corrupt penance, as I traversed West or East:
from Rome to Gaul and Dalmatia, then to Antioch,
where I had my fateful fever, my awful vision.

With leather thongs I strapped them to my back
before traveling across the Syrian deserts.
I took them on every pilgrimage, every journey,
finally sewing them into my undergarments.

They catalogue my most harrowing transgressions,
a purgatory of the fierce fires lit primarily by
the *flamma carnis*: my early manhood's passion
for feasting on exotic fruits, ripened flesh.

My diaries are the flint I strike my faith upon,
for how can I urge my monks away from sin,
if my own secret shame doesn't singe me?
I know my words are maggots swarming

a cesspool, and they hiss at me like serpents,
my lifelong detritus, these flakes of filth—
After I see Bethlehem one last time, and before
I meet Christ our Lord, I will burn them.

(Jerusalem, 419 C.E.)

Rome

The tender flesh of quail and crane.
A dolphin's heart marinated in honey,
simmered in opium, so to enhance the senses.
Platters of steaming sturgeon, wild rice
studded with olives and flowing from gourds.
Great plentitude reflected from golden goblets.
I dine again with my rich patrician friends,
their robes' purple stripes expanding like
flooded brooks as their bellies' rotundas
fill, their laughter booming.

Hedged in by troops of eunuchs,
the women blush from this surfeit of wine;
some younger ones, though just married, meet
my stare without flinching, while slowly
wetting their lips. Some let their gaze stray
up and down my body, as if daring me
to seduce them. I have eaten,
still I'm hollowed by hunger.

Rufinus, if ever I ask you to stand guard
at my door, to bar me from sin—deny me!
If ever I ask you to be a whoremaster
who steals through night to bring me
heavenly dark-haired women—
deny me!

(April 361 C.E.)

Rome

I am still imprisoned in a body.

Daily, the world tempts my flesh—
nightly I succumb.

My chest grows chaffed from
the breasts of women rubbing against it.

They scar my skin with lacquered nails,
women whose perfumed arms enflame me:

welcoming courtesans, and the slow market girls
with their trembling lower lips,

the Nubian beauties one can buy for an hour,
their genitals swollen like guava,

and from Damascus, the Hebrew whores,
breasts succulent as Persian melons,

who marvel (or pretend to) as
they mount my uncircumcised penis.

So many caverns of pleasure!
So many cravings.

Oh I am still imprisoned—
do not release me.

Desire is quenched by desire.

(September 363 C.E.)

Rome

Does the spider study Quintilian?
Does the lizard debate the toad?

What rhetoric is there for the stars?
For the laboring ants?

I, too, am born of this earth;
though I excel, I weary of grammar.

Rufinus teases me endlessly:
his beard grows thick like an aodad's,

while mine stays sparse
as a winter field.

He claims that I sleepwalk solely
to escape my lessons.

My good brother, Bonosus, disagrees,
saying I stalk the night

seeking asylum from my dreams.
There's truth in that:

last night I dreamt the divine birth—
I watched the Virgin's womb

open like a passionflower's petals
as Christ's head emerged haloed in light—

and I awoke fully aroused:
a defilement.

Tonight I'll visit the concubines again,
bathe in the moon's milky whey.

I am miserable with pleasure.

(January 364 C.E.)

Caput Mundi

"Had I a hundred tongues, a hundred lips,
A throat of iron and a chest of brass,
I could not tell men's countless sufferings." – Virgil

Rome isn't solely the "head of the world," but also
its bowels, its biceps, stomach, its Argus-eyes.
Nightly, it sleeps among its spoils, a humped monster;
by day, Rome's an uncoiling basilisk of motion and matter.
Today, on route to the Baths of Trajan, I passed through
streets thickened by outpourings of human effluvium spewed
from the *insulae*, those island tenements of utter woe.

Such awful, howling lamentations issue from their walls!
It's as if throngs of the dying are rattling their hollow bones,
their cries amplified by a thousand bullhorns' blaring.
These alleys—peopled with lepers, amputees, the pocked
faces of smallpox victims, the deformed and hobbled,
stricken castrati who rot with gangrene, mutilated slaves—
these alleys seethe with Rome's flotsam, its shame.

I held my sleeve to my nose and mouth to block the stench
and stifle my gagging, even as I warded off pickpockets,
wounded beggars, the paraffin-thin children fated to die.
A prostitute, clearly mad, bared her scabrous breasts
to me, her nipples dribbling bloody pus, her eyes wild.
A blind woman with withered arms and tattooed cheeks
was being pumped against a wall by a brawny pygmy.

Everywhere I turned, I heard the prophet of the apocalypse
proclaiming our doom, a deep roaring in my eardrums.
I stumbled from that labyrinth, sputtering with rage,
lost in a conflagration of despair. I leaned against a pillar
and retched, then wept. I swear, Christ be my witness,
that one day I'll lead my brethren from blazing Sodom,
from this horror, this fallen world.

(Rome, 371 C.E.)

Fragments from St. Jerome's Diaries

(Eastern Travels)

The seesaw of life & death,
the pulley of said and unsaid—
the pendulum that swings between
power and the hourglass—

these are the weights tipping
my mind, clamping my heart, battering
my spirit, and these the emblems of transience:
skull, candleflame, cenotaph.

*

My passion for truth's a pyre—
myself the dry kindling—
would God that I might agonize
toward purity in the mind's desert—

*

"The gourd that came up at night
and withered in a night"—
such is my fleeting life.

Death's head, the golgotha, bonehouse
of dreams: I will grate my teeth
with an iron file

to perfect my speech in Hebrew—
those holy words that buoy
me across the breach.

(Antioch, 374 C.E.)

St. Jerome in the Chalcis Desert

Sometimes the heart needs educating;
the bruise lightens to mauve,
and the strange alchemy

that turns charcoal and sap into
a raven, reverses itself into
a mendicant's shawl.

Though I seem a wizened presbyter,
dogma hounds me like a halo
of hookah smoke.

My knuckles grow hard as porphyry;
my monasticism enshrines me
in loss. I'm always cold,

anonymous as the quivering dormouse
who nightly revisits me, an oracle—
inside his mind's tiny orbit,

the universe whirls bravely.
Faith is a wagon drawn
by fireflies,

so there must be a going forth and
a going asunder, a blinding of
the mind's eye.

(Syria, 376 C.E.)

Transfigurations

Lurking in my grim sleep—an incubus,
antlered and sinister, his ur-breath toxic,
his smirk fusty, corrosive, a scythed curse.
Always unbidden, yet he comes

nearly nightly—a lewd gargoyle whose
huge scorpion tail whiplashes out at me,
whose talons drip a resinous bile, who
beheads and blasphemes, barks and bites.

Often a corpse-eyed vulture perches
upon his blistered shoulder, acidly shrieking,
"Kill the hypocrite priest and his wife!"
Then, softly, "Cursed art thou, No One."

Spiteful, shrill specter—fiendish trespasser
of my mind: he scalds me with breath-burns,
with grub teeth, glistening spittle, boggy tongue—
I can't, can't, cannot...can only sputter

muteness, erasures, silence, failure.
My heart's exhumed; its pounding resounds
a gong in my ears: Be, become what
you are not—a hospice of virtues,

a laboratory for the soul's toil,
a distillery for the essence of God
pinwheeled with light,
pinioned by mercy.

(Chalcis Desert, 377 C.E.)

Rome Again

Philo, that most erudite man among the Jews,
also navigated these streets, walking from one forum
to another, ever adrift, enthralled by this metropolis.
From bakery to brothel, from amphitheater to steamy
bathhouse, he must have strode past wheel factories,

past taverns with drunks tumbling out their doors,
past parade grounds, stadiums, and those gymnasiums
enlivened by beautiful boys oiling their torsos—past
gilt shrines and corpulent merchants' *domi*, whose
formal gardens still spill grapes, like a flood of plump

amethysts, down latticed walls. He'd have strolled
beside long aqueducts arched above rooftops, which
carry miles of arterial rivers; then he'd have circled
law courts and palaces, the Colosseum with its roaring
blood orgies, the Circus Maximus. Philo must have

descended then, down into the dankest catacombs,
where he re-entered his own mind's grotto to
chant his Hebrew psalms, to recite the Five Books,
which he knew as well as thunder's rumblings.
I shall be like an *impluvium* to his rainwater—

And would that I had been born a Jew, for in truth,
if nothing else, all my years of translation have taught
me the wisdom of Solomon's people—our faith's
great teachers—though they're misled by their rigor.
Like a wandering Jew, I'll return to Palestine,

but not until I have gathered around me,
like Moses, a tribe of ardent, penitent followers—
and they will all be young virgins and widows—
and they must serve me as pillars of purity,
as a way through the world's fires.

(Rome, 379 C.E.)

Sanctus

These women's voices shame us,
their prayers issuing from the chrysalis
of the cloister, their purity ringing its bell.

I find my monks lacking, pitiable,
marred by maleness, by a dread of heresy.
With beer-laced breath, they strain God's ears.

My legendary library, my pride, is no better
than a mausoleum: its treasured texts
chill me with worldly vanity, with allegories

aimed to instruct, but which distract me
from my vows of abstinence, poverty.
Even as I work, my *cestus* pinches my waist,

so stout I've grown from the sweets
my secretaries' wives press them to bring me.
I'm like the elephant swung by his own belly.

What a hypocrite! I watch my sisters
grow thinner in their devotions, a membrane
of holy aura hovering over their heads, and

I'm stricken with a Hades-dark mood—
for still I'm plagued, entranced by her face—
by Paula's touch—and by the body's blunt

intelligence, its thirsty tissues, swill of blood
blooming into constellations under the skin.
Still I'm enticed, allured, led astray by myself,

by my journeys toward history, by quests
for honor, fame—all earthly traps.
I will recover my lashes, my thorned whips,

unsully myself and rise from sin's sump
to the apex of sanctity. Let my penance be
two-fold: a hundred lashings, a tapeworm feast.

(Bethlehem, May 395 C.E.)

Excerpt: Letter from Bethlehem

I shudder to think of the catastrophes of our times.
For over twenty years the blood of Romans has been shed daily
between Constantinople and the Julian Alps. Thrace, Macedonia,
Dardania, Dacia, Thessaly, Achaia, Epirius, Dalmatia, Pannonias—
all sacked, pillaged, and plundered by Goths, Sarmatians, Quades
and Alans, Huns and Vandals, Marchmen.

How many of God's matrons and virgins, virtuous
and noble ladies have been violated by these brutes!
Bishops have been taken captive, priests and those in minor
orders put to death. Churches have been overthrown,
horses have been stalled by the altars of Christ,
the relics of martyrs have been dug up.

Mourning and fear abound on every side
and death appears in countless shapes and forms.

The Roman world is falling.

-Letter LX (396 C.E.)

St. Jerome in Decline

Vocatus atque non vocatus deus aderit.

Philo knew the primary creation to be spiritual,
the secondary creation earthly, of the body—
and I know the mind hovers between both
realms as an intermediary, an agent conveying
breath to substance, ideas to deed.

I pride myself on being a *vir trilinguis,*
master of three tongues, a scholar, diconate,
church Father, translator and chronicler,
historian, traveler, counselor, and theologian,
exegete and recluse, a pedagogue, librarian.

But illness breaks me, and my eyesight dims
into a wintry dusk. Like the Apostle Paul,
I still retain the skill of exhortation, but
my voice erodes and my strength abates.
Always at my sleeve now: my amanuensis,

he whose baldness reveals a fontanel
beating like a newborn's, so flung into rapt
focus is he, stylus in hand, during long dictations.
My own hand turns limaceous, though my thoughts
ripple and soar as I repeat the Psalter verses.

I've grown old. My thoughts ramble.
To us men, this life is a racecourse:
we contend here, we are crowned elsewhere.
No man can lay aside fear while serpents
beset his path. I dread impurity, but find

even in my decline, the footprints
of the devil lead my thoughts: *his strength*
is in the loins, and his force is in the navel—
thus must I make my final passage by
relinquishing all fleshly enticements.

*

These diaries record unholy ruminations—
my fatal circles of affection—but they capture
only half the man, a fresco barely penciled in:
the incomplete phantom of my contraband self,
a counter-life—intimate, dangerous as Pandora's box.

One by one, my friends have been taken from me,
my correspondents fade, then disappear into
death's grotto, and only the gentle attentions of
Melania and the younger Paula bestir me with hope.
I am overburdened, still, by the sack of Rome,

by the putrid rise of Pelagianism, by the death
of my old debater and rival, dear, feeble Rufinus.
All Christendom seems under siege, as hordes
of barbarians sweep across the Empire, the streets
crowded with battered fugitives, starving refugees.

Deprivations, burning monasteries in Bethlehem,
my estrangement from Jerusalem's Bishop—
censure and petty arguments, hindrances, panics,
derision from my clerical foes, laughable contempt.
And Paula's absence most diminishes me.

(Bethlehem, 399 C.E.)

St. Jerome's Prayer

Forgive me, Lord, for I have insinuated my sins
brutishly upon others' backs, have offended and vilified men
who crossed me verbally, have begrudged my brothers for spiritual boons
I myself lack; I have debased, despised, deformed your will with my pride.

Unbearably, at death's threshold, I will be forgiven,
as are all men and women—fallen saint, blasphemer, disbeliever,
celibate and fornicator—O forgive me for making of my longing a noose
to hang myself, swelling my limbs, flushing inside out my resolve, strangling

my holiest ambitions—Lord, forgive me the prostitution
of my pen, the effrontery of my barren soul, my circumspection
towards joy, my heart drumming like a brothel's floor, my crooked, cracked,
crass love, with its cruel-handed corruption, its grief-songs, its forked tongue—

I beg for the strength of Zeno, of Cato—for savage trials
beyond those that Job endured: the bereavements, polluted wounds,
for curses from pious friends, scorn of my superiors, sorrows so great
my tears will flood the Tiber, my name a seed trampled underfoot, my shame

my winding sheet—O Lord, I am destitute, fallen and forsaken,
a broken cistern, a breached cause, a man of bones and blood: forgive me!

(Bethlehem, circa 415 C.E.)

Last Entry

Violently the earth bucks then
buckles from underground tremors;
massive mountains shift, seas swallow coasts;
chasms wider than the Red Sea gape open;
black skies sizzle, spiked by fiery lancets:
blindingly the heavens open—

Invisibly, unutterably, my life, too,
caused my body calamity, seizures, a schism.
O monstrous my needs, petty my grievances.
I was soiled with every sinful baseness,
yet I knew that even the penitent killer
dizzily balanced on Hell's precipice
ascends to paradise—

My tongue was a rough hammer
smoothed by the elegance of secular wisdom.
Forged from granite, coal, from slag,
my heart slept for years, then erupted—
a Vesuvius of molten awe
powered by the word of God.

I have sinned and repented.
I know what light and dark bear in common:
both are passageways, doors through which
each soul pirates itself, seeking deliverance.
Let my lamentations alert you,
O listener: heed no music but
divine syllables —

Mountains beyond Mountains

We are not ignorant that marriage is honorable...
and the bed undefiled. We have read the first
decree of God: Be fruitful and multiply and
replenish the earth. But while we allow marriage,
we prefer the virginity which springs from it.
Gold is more precious than silver, but is silver,
on that account, the less silver? Is it an insult
to a tree to prefer apples to its roots or its leaves?
Is it an injury to corn to put the ear before the
stalk and the blade? As apples come from the
tree and grain from the straw, so virginity
comes from wedlock. - Letter XXXVIII

A Letter from Lea

"It was fear that first brought the gods
into the world." – Petronius Arbiter

My love,
Do you know how it feels
To live the life of a virgin?
Like a butterfly trapped
By two cupped hands.
All this week of Saturnalia,
My mother has forbidden me
To leave the house, and
Hearing the brass cymbals
And tinkling tambourines,
All the ecstatic dancing
Below my windows—
Though it's banned on
Our Christian street—
Makes me miserable.

I may only partake of
The solstice feast, says
Mother, as she sweeps her
Ostrich fan through the air.
But I yearn for you!
For not only is today the birthday
Of the Unconquerable Sun,
But it's also mine, and
There's neither solace nor joy
In feasting on silver salvers,
Nor in drinking from crystal flasks,
Nor from chinking my goblet
In honor of my life of drought.

How I miss your strong arms,
Your passion-drugged lips!
You know the old saying:
I suffer two sicknesses—
Love and Poverty—I can
Stand Poverty, but the fever
Of Love is unbearable…
I can hear you scolding me

For the irony of such
A claim. No, I'm not poor
Nor free to love, I know.

I live in this green cipollino
Marble prison, where even
The wood nymphs peopling our
Frescoes seem to smirk at me.
They, at least, though inanimate,
Dwell among laurel, ivy, and crocus,
And are slipping off their silk
Damask tunics to embrace
Their satyr lovers—
While I live my barren life
Of protected chastity.
In truth, my love, I do not
Believe in this Christ of my
Mother's, though to admit this
Would mark me as an *athinganos*.
A heretic. You see? I'm doomed.
And so might you be, for secretly
Worshipping your Mithra.

My sweet boy,
The memory of your kisses
Keeps my body alive.
At night, I burn my oil lamp
Late while I read under my covers
The *Satyricon* you sent—
Outrageous story!—but Encolpius
Only leads me to hollow pleasures.
I'd rather drink deeply
The aphrodisiac of your lips,
Kneel before your altar—

I must go now, for Mother
Calls me. I wear the pearl
Headband you sent with
My slave, Lavinia.
Here's an opaque aphorism
My dead Father used to say,
And which I send to you now
For consolation:

There are mountains
Beyond the mountains.
I am sixteen today.

(December 20, 374 C.E.)

A Letter from Rufina

Dear Paula, my good mother—
I will answer your questions truthfully—

Yes, I blame him for my sister Eusto's marriage
to Christ, and for Blesilla's awful mortification

of her flesh, her severe fasting—her early nuptial
to death. He'll never claim little Paulina!

Nor me—for though you left us bereft, alone
on the docks of Portus, Toxo's tiny voice teary

as we begged you not to abandon us for
Hieronymus— I will *never* join your virgins.

It's enough, two years having passed, that I
traveled two continents to see you again,

mother—you who were once the envy of every
Aventine lady, whose poverty alarms me.

*

In truth, I couldn't bear to attend your pious rituals
any longer: six months I'd lived at your convent—

and seen how impure thoughts seared through all
your ceremonies of devotion; saw how blind

you and he are to the other's despair over
flesh and its extreme fires, its abrogations.

*

Hieronymus is too fierce a penitent;
mother, you've martyred your life and wealth

to a ranting zealot. And for what?
For the pittance of pleasure gained from

mending his thongs, from correcting his
faltering Greek, his schoolboy Aramaic,

from exerting abstemious behavior
to blot out your grief—

*

Mother, *he's* the one privileged by your saintly
presence, not otherwise: oh, blighted man—

he tries futilely to unloosen his love for you
by filling his dank monastery with hymns,

by mutilating himself—(yes, I too glimpsed
his massacred chest that day you bathed him)—

*

I couldn't endure this travesty of faith you
both play out like old tragedians on a stage;

I couldn't suffer another day of stifled desires
that course through your rooms like an odor

of sweat mixed with honey and lye—couldn't
abide the sour denials, the furious prayers.

*

Love, mother, will never spare us from
ourselves, nor can it redeem the soul

that's fettered and raked by unspent passion.
Rome seethes with skeptics, so it pleases me

to rejoin the milling crowds again, to drape
my arm over a courtier's, to recover a life

left behind like the hull of a locust, to martyr
myself wholly to pleasure, with no remorse.

When you die, good mother,
I'll collect your bones like relics.

(Bethlehem, 387 C.E.)

A Letter from Paulina

Dearest Eusto, my physician urges me to follow
the doctrine of signatures, to eat the amnion that
webbed the blue head of my poor, dead infant,
so to spawn in myself a kind of inverse rebirth.
But I'm wracked by doubts. Another miscarriage,
yet another orphaned soul I've sent like a caterwaul
to join the oyster-colored angels, the heaving hosts.

How our pear tree's laden branches weigh me down.

Sister, the Persians call the dandelion a "messenger"
bearing good news from an unknown land, but I say
it's the exultant crown of this sunflower you sent me
that, like God's ablest charioteer, heartens me now.

My husband Pammachius knows that I'm dying—
O how am I to console him? Tell me, tell me!

Already I see how a film of sacred vapors begins
to enclose his world. Soon, he'll surrender our life
of pleasure to forever join his vows to Christ's.
Though he's a paragon of virtues, I weep for him,
knowing my death will harness him like an ox to
sorrow— Please comfort him, pray for him that
he might pursue a life of perfection as you do.

My fever makes me feral—my world turns murky,
and my face in the mirror looks like a jackal's.
My candle wick sputters as its flame devours
a fallen moth. I am that moth. I burn, a lustrum.

(Rome, August 395 C.E.)

Eustochium at Prayer

All flesh is grass and all the goodliness thereof
is as the flower of the field. – Isaiah, xl.6

Matins

God who ignites in the boundless blue
the tilting worlds whirling, the torch
of suns, incandescent vapors—all these
mirror your face diamonding the dewdrop—

Terce

and as your Spirit lights the lamps
hung above the horizon, a rain shower
softens the sun's altar, awakens my
soul's longing to open like a bud—

Sext

The Book of Hours is a house I inhabit,
house of the poor, of a humbled servant.
May my shorn hair harbor a nest of angels,
my mouth eat of your golden flesh.

None

Emblazoned is my heart with God's word.
Flames of love sear my veins, my tongue.
Let my body be a highway for rapture,
my mind homeless as the wind—

Vespers

Dusk and the evening star spills over
the hills of Bethlehem. Here was he
born, his manger dusted with the same
light pouring down its sorrow for man—

Nocturns

It is always night within the soul's breast.
A full moon reflects my naked yearning.
I am stretched like a rope across the river
of God's sanctity—I pray for strength.

(Bethlehem, 418 C.E.)

A Letter from the Abbess Eustochium

Many waters cannot quench love,
neither can the floods drown it. – Canticles 7:7

They are both gone now. Our earthly mother, my spiritual father.
How I miss them! Their devout & feverish ways.
In her dwindling hours, our devoted Paula grew
clairvoyant—somehow knowing

that Jerome would survive her lingering death
by these long years, would carry on as if in exile.
Our tormenting debt to Christ
they wove into a flaming cord of love.

Today, brother, our monastery, convent, & sanctuary
echo like empty vessels, despite the crowds
of believers and penitents, the new novitiates
who reverently throng every hall & nave.

Some say Jerome was a *nabis*, a prophet;
others deride him, I'm told, for his severity
of mood & habit. Such unsettling furies
frequented him these late autumn months.

Yet he was a tender steward to me, even though
a stern one. The witnessing stones can attest to
his greatness & to his pain, which, as you know,
I have alluded to in my earlier letters.

Though his brilliant faith & erudition commanded
his outer life, I knew something about what claimed
his interior sphere—and perhaps you, too,
suspected a wildness therein?

Earthly love offers only endless struggle, brother,
& it teaches us how soft the clay whereof we're made—
it shapes us into blunt-edged slaves—
it drags us down into the muck of sin—

But enough of these matters. Your fine girl & my niece,
        Paula, grows tall as a royal palm, & her sweetness
                carries her grandmother's voice, bears our mother
                        Paula's grace of limb & timbre.

Like the yellow-rayed coreopsis, she blooms,
        regardless of drought or torrent. Her virtues glow,
                a golden honeycomb, & a virgin she remains,
                        cleaving solely to her Scriptures.

Soon she'll take the veil, accept as her own
        His crown of thorns, crucify everything within herself
                that isn't pure, sacred, blessed by God—
                        She sends her tidings with my own—

(Bethlehem, 421 C.E.)

A Letter from the Abbess Paula the Younger

The days of man are but as grass; for he flourisheth as a flower of the field. For as soon
as the wind goeth over it, it is gone: and the place thereof shall know it no more. -Psalm 103

Dearest Cousin,
I have found among our deceased spiritual grandfather's effects
several codices bound in twine and goat leather,
and greatly damaged by the hungry meanderings of white ants,
by inclement storage, and—I suspect—by secreted tears.

I am shocked by the stark revelations
from these tawdry looking, embattled, filth-covered, embittered diaries.
Apostasy threatens their author; a barbarism of the mind
overcomes his wisdom, and a crucified spirit's tortured ravings
infiltrate their pages.

We thought we knew the man: we did not.
Could not have. So much within our hearts howls for forgiveness,
withers us, while Lucifer stands ever ready to entice us,
to harvest our sins. Jerome's private pen stuttered and
raged self-calumny, even as his public letters proved him righteous.

There is too much mystery in man,
as in the Eternal. Too great a hydra, this person to whom
our grandmother wed her life and her soul. In them both, earthly love—
that euphoria, that dread which ravishes—vied with divine love.
I grew up in the humid greenhouse of their devotion.

What to do with these diaries?
I believe their famed author would have me burn them.
Indeed, I've taken the liberty of destroying three pages which
alluded to our Elder Paula serving as an *agapeta* to Jerome—yes,
believe it!—as his priestly mistress!

I also put to flame several salacious pages
recounting how he lay with two licentious nuns—a triangulation
of orgiastic fumblings worthy (you'd remind me) of those oversexed tales
of Bacchus and of Sappho's sultry lovers on Lesbos—
Scandalous such outpourings. His fantasies saddened me.

So the scales have fallen from my unworldly eyes.
I see now, Cousin, how futilely we strive against our natures:

we desire what is alien to us, otherworldly, other than ourselves—
and such yearning tonsures our souls' wings. God lurks
behind and beyond our mirrors—

We struggle like flies to escape this vortex of sins.
We live in exile from our physical bodies.
Slumbering bears, we hibernate inside our deaths,
dreamless, waiting to be reborn again.
We stand facing God, our mouths agape.

Assyrian, African, Jew and Egyptian, even the loin-
clothed Brāhman and chanting Buddhist of whom Jerome spoke
in his letters—anchorite or centurion, Essene or harlot—what we want,
both in the kingdom of man and in the promise of heaven, is *transcendence*,
a harmony of breath with the divine—

A rebel angel he was, Cousin.
Bless Jerome's bones. Bless Paula's long-dried tears.
Herein I enclose the remainder of his writings.
Your faithful servant and friend,
chaste bride of Christ,
Paula.

(Bethlehem, circa 440 C.E.)

ENDNOTES

I have interspersed within Jerome and Paula's stories direct quotations drawn from his voluminous *Letters*. I have *italicized* those lines and passages that contain verbatim excerpts from his letters. My primary source for the English translations of Jerome's *Letters* was *A Select Library of Nicene and Post-Nicene Fathers of the Christian Church, Second Series, Volume VI: St. Jerome: Letters and Select Works*, translated by W.H. Fremantle, G. Lewis, and W.G. Martley (James Parker & Co., Oxford, 1893).

Other sources I relied upon for relevant historical, theological, and cultural information, especially regarding early Christianity and late Roman antiquity, include: *Saint Jerome in the Renaissance*, Eugene T. Rice, Jr. (Johns Hopkins University Press, 1985); *Pierpaolo Vergerio the Elder and Saint Jerome: An Edition and Translation of Sermones pro Sancto Hieronymo*, John M. McManamon, S.J. (Arizona Center for Medieval and Renaissance Studies, Tempe, 1999); *Collected Works of Erasmus, Volume 61*, edited, translated, and annotated by James F. Brady and John C. Olin (University of Toronto Press, Toronto, 1992); *Late Antiquity*, G.W. Bowersock, Peter Brown, and Oleg Grabar (Harvard University Press, 1999); *Ancient Rome and the Roman Empire*, Michael Kerrigan (Dorling Kindersley, 2001); *Handbook to Life in Ancient Rome*, Lesley Adkins and Roy A. Adkins (Oxford University Press, 1998); *Ancient Rome: Monuments Past and Present*, R.A. Staccioli (Vision Publishers, 2000); and *God: A Biography*, Jack Miles (Alfred A. Knopf, 1995).

"Father of Punctuation" – I confer this title on St. Jerome for his role in attempting to standardize the use of punctuation marks in sacred texts.

"A Celestial Salaam" – The poem's epigraph is from *Letter XXII*. I've changed the poem's italicized text, drawn from Jerome's *Letter*, from first to third person.

"St. Jerome the Hermit" – "O how often, when I was living in the sun-scorched solitude of the desert, which offers monks a savage hospitality, how often I imagined myself back among the pleasures of Rome." – *Letter XXII*, paragraph 7. The poem's epigraph is quoted in *Letter LII*, paragraph 1.

"The Vision" – *Eudaimonia*, from the Greek, means "well-being," as well as "happiness."

"St. Jerome Among the Widows" – "He who has bathed in Christ once has no need of a second bath," and "A shining skin shows a sin-stained soul." – *Letter CXVII*, paragraph 6.

"St. Jerome Alone" – *Letter CVIII*, one of Jerome's longest letters, seeks to console Eustochium on the recent loss of her mother. The letter includes this inscription Jerome wrote and had cut on Paula's tomb: *Within this tomb a child of Scipio lies,/ A daughter of the far-famed Pauline house,/ A scion of the Gracchi, of the stock/Of Agamemnon's self, illustrious:/Here rests the lady Paula, well-beloved/Of both her parents, with Eustochium/ For daughter; she the first of Roman dames/Who hardship chose and Bethlehem for Christ.*

"Bethlehem (387 C.E.)" – "adultery of the tongue" is from *Letter XXII*, paragraph 29; "What honey is sweeter..." is a quotation from Matthew 14:25-33 which Jerome uses in *Letter XXX*.

"A Nocturne" – The poem's epigraph appears in *Letter XLVII*, paragraph 19. A *cornu* (Latin: horn) was a circular trumpet of ancient Rome, of Etruscan origin, and is similar to a modern French horn.

"A Matriarch of Rome" – *Dum spiro spero*: "As long as I breathe, I hope." Many thanks to John Felstiner from Stanford University for bringing this anonymous quotation to my attention.

"Obiter Dictum" – The poem's title, from the Latin, means "an aside."

"The Lost Diaries" – *In girum imus nocte et consumimur igni*: "In circles we go in the night and are consumed by fire." I'm indebted to French composer, Phillipe Bodin, for teaching me this wonderful aphoristic Latin palindrome.

"Paula's Circle" – A *stola* is an ancient Roman dress; a *pallium* is an outer cloak.

"Remus" – In Roman mythology, Remus is the twin brother of Romulus, the eponymous co-founder of Rome. The sons of Mars and the vestal virgin Rhea Sylvia, the twins were suckled by a she-wolf after their mother was condemned to death for breaking her vows of chastity. As adults, the twins founded Rome, and Romulus eventually killed Remus during an argument over the placement of city walls. (In 2008 archeologists discovered in Rome a vaulted cavern believed to be the Lupercale shrine, the sacred place where the legendary wolf nursed the twin boys.)

"St. Paula Among the Marigolds" – The ecstatic lines in this poem's last stanza were influenced by a poem entitled "The Classic" by Polish poet Wislawa Szymborska.

"Excerpts: Letters from Bethlehem" – Terence (Publius Terentius Afer, c. 185?-159 B.C.E.) was a great Roman satirist. Born in Carthage, he came to Rome as a slave, and was educated and later freed by a Roman senator. The second quotation's reference to the personified Jerusalem's "feet" was a commonly used euphemism for genitals in the Old Testament.

"Caput Mundi" – The epigraph from Virgil appears in *Letter LX*, paragraph 16.

"Fragments from St. Jerome's Diaries" – The quotation in the fourth stanza is from Jonah 4:6-10. *Golgotha* means "skull" in Aramaic.

"Rome (363 C.E.)" – "Desire is quenched by desire." – *Letter XXII,* paragraph 17.

"Rome (364 C.E.)" – An *aodad* is a wild sheep from North Africa with curved horns and a long beard.

"Transfigurations" – The last line in the third stanza echoes several lines in poems by Paul Celan, especially those in "There Was Earth Inside Them, And They Dug" and "Psalm." (Translations by John Felstiner from *Selected Prose & Poetry of Paul Celan,* W.W. Norton, 2000.)

"Rome Again (379 C.E.)" – An *impluvium* is a receptacle used in ancient Rome to collect rainwater. Philo Judeas (c. 30 B.C.E. – 40 C.E.) was a Jewish philosopher from the Alexandrian School, and the most significant thinker during Hellenistic Judaism. In *Letter LXX* (paragraph 3), Jerome refers to him as a man "...whom critics call the Jewish Plato." Philo coined the term "polytheism."

"St. Jerome in Decline" – The translation from the Latin of the epigraph is: "Bidden or not bidden, God is present." This axiom was inscribed over Carl Jung's front door in Zurich, and on his tombstone. Pelagianism is a doctrine which asserted that human will is capable of good without the assistance of divine grace. Its main proponent, Pelagius, was a contemporary and bitter enemy of Jerome's. The Church eventually condemned the doctrine as heresy. The italicized lines in stanza 5 and 6 are from *Letter XXII,* paragraph 3.

"Excerpt: Letter from Bethlehem" – Jerome uses another quotation from Virgil in this passage.

"St. Jerome's Prayer" – Zeno "the Phoenician" (334-262 B.C.E.) was a famous stoic who committed suicide in extreme old age. Cato of Utica killed himself after the battle of Thapsus (46 B.C.E.) to avoid falling into Caesar's hands.

"A Letter from Lea" – The celebration of the Roman solstice festival, Saturnalia, was banned in 375 C.E. Mithraism was one of the chief rival religions to Christianity during late Roman antiquity. It involved the worship of the Indo-Persian god of light, *Mithra* (Sanskrit: Mitra), and its followers worshipped in a chapel called a Mithraeum. The quotation in the third stanza, which begins, *"I suffer two sicknesses—"* is an anonymous axiom drawn from Kenneth Rexroth's translations of *Poems from the Greek Anthology* (University of Michigan Press, 1962). Petronius Arbiter (b.?-d.66 C.E.) was a Roman poet and satirist, as well as a governor of Bithynia, and the reputed author of *Satryicon,* the first western European novel. Suspected of conspiring against Nero, Petronius was forced by the Emperor to commit suicide. The name of Encolpius (*Satyricon's* roguish, voluptuary hero) has been translated both as "the Embracer," and as "the Crotch."

"A Letter from Paulina" – The "doctrine of signatures" was one which held that a quality embodied in a drug engenders the same quality in the body (e.g., the use of bulls' testicles as an aphrodisiac).

"Eustochium at Prayer" – In Jerome's time, the seven canonical hours of prayer had not yet been finally fixed, hence this poem's six hours, or intervals, of prayer.

"A Letter from the Abbess Paula the Younger" – By the 2nd and 3rd centuries C.E. the codex—a collection of papyrus sheets fastened by a spine and usually bound in protective covers—had become the common book form for Greek literature and the Christian Bible. Jewish scriptures were still inscribed and preserved on rolled papyrus or parchment scrolls. (Colin H. Roberts and T.C. Skeat, *The Birth of the Codex*, Oxford University Press, London, 1983). *Agapetae* (from the Greek: "beloved ones") were women who lived with unmarried clergy as spiritual sisters, but who apparently, in many cases, also lived with them as mistresses. Jerome mentions them in *Letter XXII*, paragraph 14.

Afterword by Chris Abani

Maurya Simon's *The Raindrop's Gospel* is a many faceted gem. A fair mix of the novel-verse-genre, it calls to the epic tradition and yet trembles with all the veiled passion of Solomon's Songs and David's Psalms. It bravely takes on the "possible" romance between two saints of the early Christian church with all the sensual power of Rumi loving God and the beautiful fragility of Jeff Buckley singing Hallelujah. These poems are songs to humanity and its pain, the terrible but awe-inspiring failure of the body to be whipped into the course of the religion's understanding of the divine and its will.

In these poems that hover somewhere between the lyric and the narrative, between aubade and the troubadour's song and the griot's incantatory orature, between Virgil's joy and Horace's reasoned arguments, Simon charts a path of transformation and possibility, where the true redemption is the realization that all love is light. This baptism is for the soul to accept that the body will be divine but only on its own terms, and this is not shame, this is not sin. Scholars of American literature will hear all the echoes of Hawthorne's "The Scarlet Letter" and its cautionary note, one that Chaucer sounds against Bunyan's "Pilgrim's Progress," the caution, relevant in our times, is that the idea of purity, and any attempts to force it, is the true tyranny. In this way, Simon's book echoes the message that has been spooling through history every time the profane and the divine collide; a ripple across the soul's calm.

Feminist, heretical, apocryphal, theological, inspirational, this book is as much about art and the artist's attempt to render the ineffable as it is about the specificity of the lives of the two saints. Even its take on feminism is heretical. Instead of attempting an alternative construction of the strong female, the book comes at this politics from the position of the male, underpinning the fragility of masculinity, and thus emphasizing so beautifully the strength of women.

There are countless memorable lines and passages, but here are a few selected ones (it is important to say that in this book, the stanzas emulate the true meaning of their name, which in Italian means rooms, and this book's embedded architecture is that of the many domains and domiciles of the soul on its journey to life and back to the silence of God, and emulates Christ's adage):

(From *Father of Punctuation*)

> In moments between preoccupations, in those pauses
> punctured by the sound of malm being ground up
> by bricklayers, or by the scolding magpies, or by
>
> Paula praying quietly with her garnet beads –
> the click and suspirations – he swabs his brow and
> thinks about what sets apart one interval from another:

how a specific point must be molded into significance;
how each phase of an Idea must be syncopated, or
rotated, isolated or expanded, until its complexity

rings as clear as brook water enshrined in a chalice.

(From: *The Miracle*)

His once porcelain teeth have turned a mottled gray; his nails
look like graphite; the skin on his hands grows loose, flaccid;
his eyes go blank, his mind hemmed in, paralyzed by prayer.

(From: *St. Jerome's Dreams (II)*)

And he awoke, drenched in sweat, and began
to strum and pummel his sex that thrust

its club upwards, clawing his skin raw, while
the coterie of wanton women still writhed

transparently upon him, bringing him now to
the edge of madness, until at last he broke

open, his seed spilling in throbs on his groin.
Spent, he lifted the crucifix from his neck

and jabbed it into his brow, stabbing it
over and over into his sin...

(From: *A Nocturne*)

A cobalt night and the eager, stark tutelage of the stars...

To not believe is perhaps the deeper devotion, and this book is skeptical in all the best ways, and is itself a yearning for something the poet knows cannot be contained in language. It is as Rumi says; we stand in the ocean holding a cup of water, careful not to spill any lest we lose it all: this exquisite agony is perhaps this book's greatest gift.

I would like to thank the editors of the following magazines for publishing the poems listed below in their pages, though sometimes in slightly different form, or with earlier titles:

Agenda: Remus, St. Jerome Alone; *Colorado Review*: A Nocturne; *The Gettysburg Review*: St. Jerome among the Widows, St. Jerome's Dreams (I), St. Jerome's Dreams (II); *Great River Review*: St. Jerome's Prayer; *Hotel Amerika*: Eustochium and Blesilla, The Labyrinth; *Image: A Journal of the Arts & Religion*: Bethlehem (formerly "Two Saints in Bethlehem"), Eustochium at Prayer; *The Journal*: Obiter Dictum, A Letter from Rufina (formerly "Blesilla's Tale"); *The Kenyon Review*: The Spiral Pilgrimage; *The National Poetry Review*: St. Jerome's Casket; *New England Review*: Paula's Tale: Mourning; *Ploughshares*: Father of Punctuation, St. Jerome the Hermit; *Poetry*: Rome, 364 C.E. (formerly "St. Jerome in Rome"), Sanctus (formerly "St. Jerome's Sanctum"), St. Jerome in Decline; *Prairie Schooner*: St. Paula among the Marigolds, A Letter from Abbess Paula the Younger, St. Jerome's Lost Diaries, The Vision; *Smartish Pace*: A Matriarch of Rome, Translation, Invocation, St. Jerome Rests from His Labors; *The Southern Review*: Hieronymus and the Lion, Transfigurations; *32 Poems*: St. Jerome in the Chalcis Desert; *The Women's Review of Books*: The Yea Sayer, Paula's Circle.

Many thanks to Meg Files for including "St. Paula" ("Before Her Death") in the anthology, *Lasting: Poetic Visions of Aging*. My gratitude also to the National Endowment for the Arts for awarding me a Fellowship in Poetry, to the American Academy in Rome for two Visiting Artist/Scholar residencies in 2002 and 2007, and many heartfelt thanks to The MacDowell Colony and its staff, for extending its hospitality to me during two resplendent Octobers. Finally, my abundant thanks to Gray Jacobik, Barry Sanders, Jack Miles, Peggy Shumaker, Wendy Herbert, Chris Abani, Barbara Goldberg, Michael Collier, Cynthia Tuell, my soul sister, Helène Aylon, my former UCR colleague and fellow Jerome enthusiast, Professor Andrew Jacobs, and to B.H. (Pete) Fairchild, upon whose literary and aesthetic acumen I have relied repeatedly. Finally, I thank Naomi Falk and Leah Falk Diaz, my daughters, and my grandsons, Alex and Ethan—my heart's lifelines.

Poetry Titles from Elixir Press

Circassian Girl
by Michelle Mitchell-Foust

Imago Mundi
by Michelle Mitchell-Foust

Distance From Birth by Tracy Philpot

Original White Animals by Tracy Philpot

Flow Blue by Sarah Kennedy

A Witch's Dictionary by Sarah Kennedy

Monster Zero by Jay Snodgrass

Drag by Duriel E. Harris

Running the Voodoo Down
by Jim McGarrah

Assignation at Vanishing Point
by Jane Satterfield

The Jewish Fake Book
by Sima Rabinowitz

Recital by Samn Stockwell

Murder Ballads by Jake Adam York

Floating Girl (Angel of War)
by Robert Randolph

Puritan Spectacle by Robert Strong

Keeping the Tigers Behind Us
by Glenn J. Freeman

Bonneville by Jenny Mueller

Cities of Flesh and the Dead
by Diann Blakely

The Halo Rule by Teresa Leo

Perpetual Care by Katie Cappello

Prelude to Air from Water
by Sandy Florian

Let Me Open You A Swan
by Deborah Bogen

Fiction titles

How Things Break by Kerala Goodkin

Nine Ten Again by Phil Condon

Limited Edition Chapbooks

Juju by Judy Moffat

Grass by Sean Aden Lovelace

X-testaments by Karen Zealand

Rapture by Sarah Kennedy

Green Ink Wings by Sherre Myers

Orange Reminds You Of Listening
by Kristin Abraham

In What I Have Done & What I Have Failed To Do by Joseph P. Wood

Hymn of Ash by George Looney

Bray by Paul Gibbons